500 BOWLS
Contemporary Explorations
of a Timeless Design

500 BOWLS

Contemporary Explorations
of a Timeless Design

LARK BOOKS

A Division of Sterling Publishing Co., Inc.
New York

EDITOR: **Suzanne J. E. Tourtillott**
ART DIRECTOR: **Kathleen Holmes**
COVER DESIGNER: **Barbara Zaretsky**
PRODUCTION ASSISTANCE: **Shannon Yokeley**
EDITORIAL ASSISTANCE: **Rosemary Kast**

Library of Congress Cataloging-in-Publication Data

10 9 8 7 6 5 4 3 2 1

First Edition

Published by Lark Books, a division of
Sterling Publishing Co., Inc.
387 Park Avenue South, New York, N.Y. 10016

© 2003, Lark Books

Distributed in Canada by Sterling Publishing, c/o Canadian Manda Group,
One Atlantic Ave., Suite 105 Toronto, Ontario, Canada M6K 3E7

Distributed in the U.K. by Guild of Master Craftsman Publications Ltd., Castle
Place, 166 High Street, Lewes, East Sussex, England BN7 1XU Tel: (+ 44) 1273
477374, Fax: (+ 44) 1273 478606, Email: pubs@thegmcgroup.com, Web:
www.gmcpublications.com

Distributed in Australia by Capricorn Link (Australia) Pty Ltd., P.O. Box 704,
Windsor, NSW 2756 Australia

If you have questions or comments about this book, please contact:

Lark Books
67 Broadway
Asheville, NC 28801
(828) 253-0467

Manufactured in China

CONTENTS

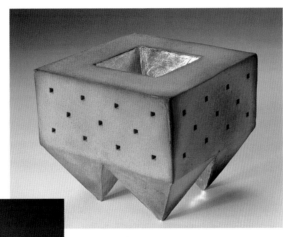

INTRODUCTION

"...a testament to the ceaseless well of creativity and inventiveness that is contained within each of us."

What makes the bowl so enduring? Obviously, it is the functional object par excellence. It can be both useful and decorative. It has everything: form, volume, surface, texture, and color. The bowl is both simple and complex. It can be, at once, deeply personal and yet it can also convey deep metaphysical insights. It is simultaneously mysterious and transparent. While the exterior is obvious, the interior conceals its form and content. Only when the viewer draws closer is that space revealed. That is when we are often surprised by a magical interior that was hidden inside a calm exterior, or vice versa.

The bowl is one of the simplest and most basic forms that potters make. According to archaeologists, it may also be the first functional ceramic object ever made. The accidental burning of clay-lined baskets over 10,000 years ago is believed to have created the first ceramic bowl.

John Britt
Oil Spot Bowl, 2002

8 x 5 x 8 in. (20.3 x 12.7 x 20.3 cm)
Iron-stain grolleg porcelain; cone 10 oxidation; cone 10 reduction
Photo by artist

You may think that after 10,000 years of history, there is nothing new to say with a bowl; at least nothing that has not already been said a thousand times before. But the 500 bowls presented in this book prove otherwise. They prove that there is still a lot to be said, felt, and expressed in the bowl, and that the bowl is still being reinterpreted and reinvented every day.

One of the first successful forms I ever made on the potter's wheel was a small bowl. I distinctly remember opening the spinning wet lump of clay with a small wooden rib and the bowl was magically born, almost without effort. That was a pivotal moment that changed my life forever. I fell in love with forming objects on the wheel. I fell in love with the malleability of clay, its yielding. In the bowl I found a love of form and symmetry. This led me to an investigation of ceramic history, culture, and ancient traditions, which in turn sent me on a study of materials, geography, geology, and the chemical systems that make ceramics possible. Little did I know that, just as a bowl opens when the wooden rib is placed inside it, so, too, a whole new amazing world opened to me in that spinning lump of clay on the potters wheel some 17 years ago.

Having selected these 500 bowls from the many entries submitted, I am amazed at the mastery of ceramic processes and chemistry displayed in union with unique personal artistic visions. Every technique from across the globe and through centuries of time is presented here. Judy Motzkin's pit-fired bowl is a wonderful continuation of the traditions of the earliest potters. Holly Walker has taken slip and earthenware traditions to new levels with her own intuitive vision.

Of course, the Italian tradition of majolica is well represented, particularly in Posey Bacopoulos's wonderful bowls. The long rich history of wood-fired work is exemplified in Dale Huffman's beautiful natural ash piece. And the tradition of porcelain is highlighted by both Greg Daly's colorful bowls and the quiet elegance of Meredith Brickell's simple forms.

John Britt
Faceted Copper Red Bowl, 1999

6 x 8 x 7 in. (15.2 x 20.3 x 17.8 cm)
Grolleg porcelain; cone 10 reduction
Photo by artist

The vast array of styles and techniques presented here is a tribute to past cultures and the unquenchable creativity of the human spirit. This book reflects a world that is becoming smaller and smaller. The technological revolution has given us access to more ideas, visual objects, and ceramic technology than ever before. As a result of mass communication the world is learning, sharing, and blending together. From this blending comes new views, new possibilities, and new aesthetic choices.

The amazing beauty and variety in *500 Bowls* is a testament to the ceaseless well of creativity and inventiveness that is contained within each of us. There is an unstoppable need to experiment, innovate and push the limits of the known world. *500 Bowls* is meant to inspire those who read it to find and express their own unique artistic vision.

John Britt

THE BOWLS

Lynne McCarthy
Yellow Peace, 2001

4 x 6 x 6½ in. (10.2 x 15.2 x 16.5 cm)
Pinched raku; paddled; terra sigillata; copper wire; banana
peels; leaves; single-fired saggar-fired cone 04 electric
Photo by Michael Noa

*I love saggar and pit firings, especially
the idea of giving up a piece to the
organic materials and smoke for decoration. The pieces always seem so
quiet and peaceful to me.*

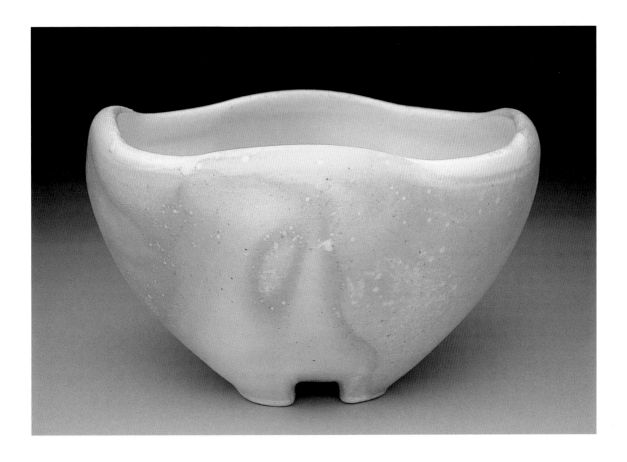

Missy M. McCormick
Carved Serving Bowl in Soft Blue, 2001

5½ x 9½ x 6½ in. (14 x 24.1 x 16.5 cm)
Wheel-thrown stoneware; altered; carved; flashing slip;
matte blue glaze; bisque cone 06;
soda cone 11 cross-draft kiln

Kate Maury
Bowl, 2001

6 x 9 x 9 in. (15.2 x 22.9 x 22.9 cm)
Wheel-thrown porcelain; glaze soda cone 10
Photo by Marty Springer and Bill Wikrent

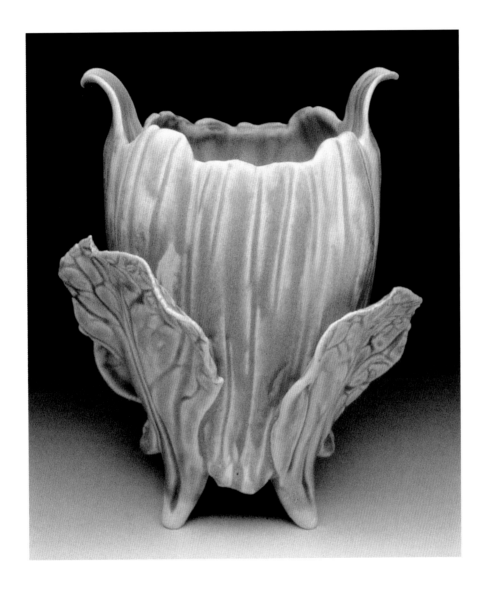

Bonnie Seeman
Yellow and Pink Bowl with Leaves, 2001

6 x 5½ x 5½ in. (15.2 x 14 x 14 cm)
Wheel-thrown and altered porcelain; hand-built;
bisque 1873°F (1023°C); glaze cone 10, oxidation
Photo by artist

Bryan Hiveley
Green/Yellow Bowl, 2002

Coil built; layered low-fire glazes; glaze cone 04

Aase Haugaard

Bowls, 2001

Left: 5⅛ x 5½ in. (13 x 14 cm); right: 5⅛ x 6¹⁄₁₆ in. (13 x 15.5 cm)
Wheel thrown and altered; shino; terra sigillata slips;
cone 10 wood

Susan B. Goldstein
Tri-Layered Bowl: "Sunrise in Kentucky"

14 x 18 x 18 in. (35.6 x 45.7 x 45.7 cm)
Layered and draped slabs; sprayed Mason stains;
single-fired cone 04
Photo by Jeff Rogers

Sandra Byers

Overlapping Layers, 2001

1¾ x 3¼ x 3½ in. (4.4 x 8.3 x 8.9 cm)
Pinched and carved porcelain; lightly glazed; bisque
cone 04; cone 9½ electric, controlled cooling
Photo by artist

*A fragment of a shell picked up on a
beach can turn into an inspiration.*

Suze Lindsay
Pedestal Bowl, 1999

11 x 12½ x 4 in. (27.9 x 31.8 x 10.2 cm)
Wheel-thrown and altered stoneware; assembled;
slips; glazes; glaze salt cone 10
Photo by Tom Mills

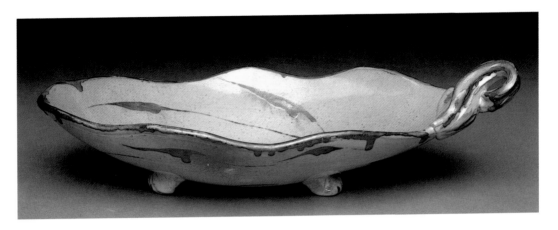

Marilyn Dennis Palsha

Footed Leaf Fruit Bowl, 2001

5 x 17 x 8 in. (12.7 x 43.2 x 20.3 cm)
Slab-built red earthenware; majolica; airbrushed
stains, oxides; bisque cone 03; glaze cone 03
Photo by Seth Tice-Lewis

Steven Roberts

3 Bowls, 1999

4 in. (10.2 cm) high
Wheel-thrown and altered porcelain;
glaze cone 10

Marilyn Richeda
Spotted Bowl, 2001

$3\frac{1}{2}$ x 5 x 5 in. (8.9 x 12.7 x 12.7 cm)
Wheel-thrown red earthenware; speckled glaze;
Mason stains; single-fired cone 04 gas
Photo by Smith-Baer, Ltd.

Marta Matray Gloviczki
Rippled Shallow Bowl, 2001

3 x 6 x 7 in. (7.6 x 15.2 x 17.8 cm)
Hand-built porcelain; broken glass; cone 12 wood
Photo by Peter Lee

Gabriele Hain
Bowl with Three Pierced Fields, 1994

1⅜ x 3 x 3 in. (3.6 x 7.6 x 7.6 cm)
Slip-cast Limoges porcelain; pierced and carved;
blue-stained porcelain; transparent glaze; bisque 1112°F (600°C);
bisque cone 08, 1796°F (980°C); glaze cone 7, 2246°F (1230°C);
luster cone 018, 1382°F (750°C)
Photo by Franz Linschinger

Virginia Scotchie
Indigo/Bronze Knob Bowl, 2000

11 x 9 x 18 in. (27.9 x 22.9 x 45.7 cm)
Coil built; bronze, textured glazes;
glaze cone 6 oxidation
Photo by Brian Dressler

Gay Smith
Tiptoe Bowl, 2001

5½ x 8 x 6 in. (14 x 20.3 x 15.2 cm)
Porcelain; altered and faceted on wheel; added feet
and handles; raw glazed; single-fired soda cone 10
Photo by Tom Mills

Nicholas Joerling
Punch Bowl, 2000

14 x 17 x 18 in. (35.6 x 43.2 x 45.7 cm)
Wheel-thrown and altered stoneware; wax resist;
cone 10 gas, reduction
Photo by Tom Mills

Terry Gess
Large Bowl, 1999

5 x 18 x 10 in. (12.7 x 45.7 x 25.4 cm)
Wheel-thrown white stoneware; multiple slips; salt

Cynthia Bringle
Fish Bowl, 2000

15 x 11 x 5 in. (38.1 x 27.9 x 12.7 cm)
Wheel thrown and hand built; cone 10
Photo by Tom Mills

Theresa Yondo
Bowl with Sunflower Pattern, 2001

4 x 8½ x 8½ in. (10.2 x 21.6 x 21.6 cm)
Wheel-thrown porcelain; sgraffito; wax resist;
glaze cone 10 electric
Photo by Daniel Milner

Gardening was a big part of my summer activity for the year 2000. The sunflowers grew so tall and majestic. Over the winter I dried the heads in my studio. When spring rolled around and I began glazing the work I had made during the winter months, a sunflower pattern began to develop on the surface.

Stephen F. Fabrico
Bowl with Handles, 2002

7 x 16 x 14½ in. (17.8 x 40.6 x 36.8 cm)
Slab built; press molded; wheel;
carved; glaze cone 10 gas
Photo by Bob Barrett

Last fall I started playing around with leaves on my work. I walked into the studio one day and it just happened. In a few weeks all of my pots were covered in leaf designs. When I'm tired of leaves, I'll move on to something else.

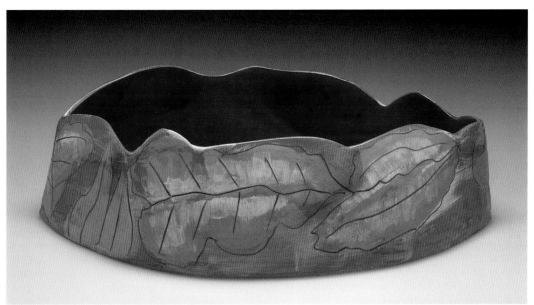

Susan Kowalczyk
Leaf Bowl (Orange), 2000

4½ x 14½ x 9½ in. (11.4 x 36.8 x 24.1 cm)
Hand-built earthenware; slips; glaze; glaze cone 03
Photo by Andrew Fortune

Lis Ehrenreich
Bluish Bowl, 1999

$9\frac{7}{8}$ x $8\frac{1}{4}$ in. (25 x 21 cm)
Wheel-thrown red Danish earthenware; stamped;
engobe decorated; bisque 1472°F (800°C);
ash/borax glaze 2156°F (1180°C); electric, reduction
Photo by Erik Balle Povlsen

Joseph Bruhin
Tea Bowl, 2001

$4\frac{1}{2}$ x 4 x $3\frac{1}{2}$ in. (11.4 x 10.2 x 8.9 cm)
Wheel-thrown porcelain; fired on side on shells;
glaze cone 11 wood
Photo by Michael Crow

Randy Edmonson

Tea Bowl, 1999

4 x 5 x 5 in. (10.2 x 12.7 x 12.7 cm)
Wheel-thrown and altered stoneware; feldspar
inclusions; glaze cones 10-12 anagama kiln
Photo by Taylor Dabney

Robert Briscoe

Noodle Bowl, 2001

3¾ x 6½ x 6½ in. (9.5 x 16.5 x 16.5 cm)
Wheel-thrown and paddled stoneware;
crackle slip; ash glaze; glaze cone 9
Photo by Wayne Torborg

Scott Lykens
Trophy Bowl, 2000

7 x 11 x 4 in. (17.8 x 27.9 x 10.2 cm)
Wheel-thrown; folded lip; altered; trimmed; slip; lay-
ered glazes; bisque cone 07; glaze cone 6 gas
Photo by artist

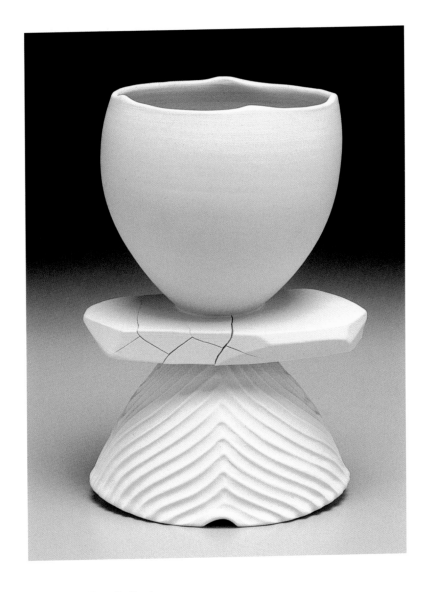

Don R. Davis
Pedestal Bowl with Slab Collar, 2000

10 x 6 x 5 in. (25.4 x 15.2 x 12.7 cm)
Wheel thrown, hand built, and carved; interior glazed;
natural porcelain exterior; cone 7 oxidation
Photo by Tim Barnwell

Lisa Goldberg
Bowls, 2001

11 x 13 x 5 in. (27.9 x 33 x 12.7 cm)
Slab-built stoneware; coil built; slip; wax resist;
glaze; glaze soda cone 10
Photo by Mel Mittermiller

Kimberly Davy
Celebration Bowl, 2002

12⅝ x 12⅝ x 7½ in. (32 x 32 x 19 cm)
Wheel-thrown porcelain; altered; sprigg mold applica-
tion with polychrome glaze; glaze cone 6
Photo by artist

Jenny Mendes
Two-Mouthed Bowl, 1998

13 x 13 x 4 in. (33 x 33 x 10.2 cm)
Slab built and slump molded; added foot; terra sigilatta;
black and white underglaze; incised drawing; cone 3
Photo by Jerry Anthony

Ricky Maldonado

Quad

5 x 11 x 16 in. (12.7 x 27.9 x 40.6 cm)
Coil-built terra cotta; slip; glaze dots; glaze cone 06
Photo by Image-Ination

Karen Jennings
Edge, 1999

7⅞ x 14⅛ x 14⅛ in. (20 x 36 x 36 cm)
Press-molded grogged white stoneware; hand built;
colored engobes; crawling glaze; glaze cone 6
Photo by Ian Hobbs

Una Mjurka
Carrot Bowl #1, 2002

6 x 18 x 13 in. (15.2 x 45.7 x 33 cm)
Hand built; layered engobes; oxide; glaze washes;
glaze multi-fired cones 06-04
Photo by artist

The idea for these pieces was drawn from a larger body of work. For the past few years I've been focusing on elaborate still lifes of fruit and vegetables. In this exploration I have deviated from my more straightforward compositions to incorporating vegetables as structural elements in functional ware.

Victor Greenaway

"Bucchero" Tall Bowl Forms, 2002

Left: 6¹¹/₁₆ x 5³/₈ in. (17 x 15 cm);
right: 6¹/₄ x 6¹/₄ in. (16 x 16 cm)
Wheel-thrown and altered terra cotta;
lightly polished; smoke fired in fume box

Bucchero is an ancient Etruscan technique from approximately 600 B.C.E. I was introduced to the technique in Orvieto, Italy, in 1999. The clay I used from that region is a very fine, low-temperature terra cotta. The product is a wonderful foil for my high-fired porcelain.

Kathy Ross
Jake Wilson
3-Piece Bowl, 2002

8 x 18 in. (20.3 x 45.7 cm)
Slab-built porcelain; layered glazes and overglaze;
bisque cone 05; glaze cone 10
Photo by Pat Pollard

Mark Johnson
Fluted Bowl, 2001

6 x 9 x 9 in. (15.2 x 22.9 x 22.9 cm)
Wheel-thrown and altered white stoneware; black
underglaze; wax resist; multiple glazes; soda cone 10
Photo by artist

Judith Motzkin
Cut Edge Bowl, 1999

5 x 16 x 16 in. (12.7 x 40.6 x 40.6 cm)
Wheel-thrown white earthenware; cut; terra
sigillata; cone 08 gas, saggar-fired
with combustibles
Photo by Tom Lang

*When a bowl's edges are thrown to
extremes, they sometimes call to be
squared with a knife. This one might
have been damaged along the way,
providing an opportunity to alter
and play with the form. It is always
good to look for the accident, the
mistake, or the opportunity provided
by the unexpected.*

Arlene Cason
Horsehair Raku Pedestal Bowl, 2002

6 x 15½ in. (15.2 x 39.4 cm)
Slab-built stoneware; wheel-thrown pedestal; terra sigillata;
horsehair; over-sprayed with ferric chloride; glaze cone 04 raku
Photo by Glen Luttrell

*I strive for a purity of form that will emphasize
the qualities of the clay and surface finishes.
Spare forms with quiet voices allow each element to speak for itself.*

Marty Fielding

Untitled, 2002

2 x 11½ x 11½ in. (5 x 29.2 x 29.2 cm)
Wheel-thrown stoneware; layered glazes; wax
resist; cone 11 gas, reduction
Photo by artist

*The interface and halo effect where
the glazes overlap is created by
brushing wax on a shino glaze,
then applying another glaze on top.*

Jerilyn Virden
Untitled (Double-Walled Bowl), 2001

4 x 10 x 10 in. (10.2 x 25.4 x 25.4 cm)
Coil-built dark stoneware; slab built; black glaze;
bisque cone 08; glaze cone 10
Photo by Tom Mills

Posey Bacopoulos
Long Oval Bowl, 2000

2½ x 17 x 8 in. (6.4 x 43.2 x 20.3 cm)
Slab-built terra cotta on a hump mold;
majolica; stains; glaze cone 04
Photo by D. James Dee

Joyce Nagata
Pears, 2000

6 x 20 x 12 in.
(15.2 x 50.8 x 30.5 cm)
Slab- and coil-built terra-cotta
earthenware; hump molded;
majolica; bisque cone 04
Photo by John Carlano

Lucy Breslin
Summer Song #13, 2002

10 x 15 x 11 in. (25.4 x 38.1 x 27.9 cm)
Wheel-thrown white earthenware; hand built; layered
glazes; bisque cone 07; glaze cone 04
Photo by Mark Johnson

Susan Beiner
Victorian Punch, 1999

10 x 14 x 7 in. (25.4 x 35.6 x 17.8 cm);
4½ x 4 x 3½ in. (11.4 x 10.2 x 8.9 cm)
Slip cast; assembled; multi-fired cones 6, 04, and 06;
luster cone 018

Priscilla Hollingsworth
Red Tip Bowl, 2002

Hand-built terra cotta; double walled; applied decoration; underglaze, oxide, and dark red glaze; bisque cone 04; cone 08
Photo by artist

Geoffrey Swindell

Bowl, 2002

2½ x 4½ in. (6.4 x 11.4 cm)
Wheel-thrown and slip-cast porcelain; glaze cone 7
Photo by Tom Swindell

Norma Price

Snow Gums—Motionless Movement, 2000

Left: 7⅞ x 10⅝ x 7⅞ in. (20 x 27 x 20 cm);
right: 7⅞ x 9 ½ x 7⅞ in. (20 x 24 x 20 cm)
Wheel-thrown and altered porcelain; terra sigillata,
glazed interiors; glaze cone 8 oxidation
Photo by Matt Kelso

*These still, asymmetrical forms were
inspired by the twisted limbs of the snow
gums, whose leaves are constantly blown
by the winds of the Australian high country.*

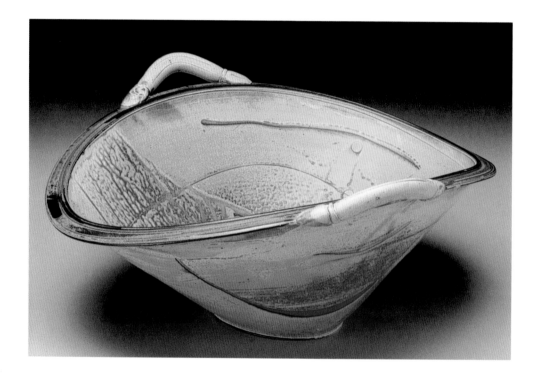

Nicholas Joerling
Large Bowl, 2001

11 x 16 x 17 in. (27.9 x 40.6 x 43.2 cm)
Wheel-thrown and altered stoneware; wax resist; cone 10 gas, reduction
Photo by Tom Mills

Stephen Heywood
Two Faceted Bowls, 2000

5 x 6 x 4 in. (12.7 x 15.2 x 10.2 cm)
Wheel-thrown stoneware; cone 10 wood
Photo by artist

Harriet E. Ross
Untitled, 1999

5 x 7 x 5 in. (12.7 x 17.8 x 12.7 cm)
Wheel thrown; glaze cone 10 reduction
Photo by James Dee

Anne Lloyd
Cat and Dog Heaven, 1996

8 x 10 in. (20.3 x 25.4 cm)
Slab and press-molded raku; modeled figures
Photo by John Carlano

Bonnie Baer
Untitled, 2001

4 x 6 x 6 in. (10.2 x 15.2 x 15.2 cm)
Slab construction white raku; Barnard slip;
oxides; glaze cone 04
Photo by Michael Noa

Carole Ann Fer
Condiment Bowl, 2002

3 x 5 x 3½ in. (7.6 x 12.7 x 8.9 cm)
Wheel-thrown porcelain; altered; feet, lugs
added; sgraffito; appliquéd button; copper slip;
semi-matte glaze; glaze cone 6 oxidation
Photo by Ken Woisard

Kimberly Davy
Bowl and Pedestal, 2001

$6^{11}/_{16}$ x $5^{1}/_{8}$ x $4^{3}/_{8}$ (17 x 13 x 11 cm)
Wheel-thrown porcelain; altered;
polychrome glaze; glaze cone 6
Photo by artist

Randy Borchers
Pooka Ness
Tomato Bowl, 2001

6 x 6 ½ in. (15.2 x 16.5 cm)
Wheel-thrown stoneware; carved; glazed;
bisque cone 06; glaze cone 9
Photo by Peter Lee

Elk Hollow Pottery is the collaborative team of Randy Borchers and Pooka Ness. Pooka sculpts her designs onto Randy's wheel-thrown pieces.

Ruchika Madan

Fruit Bowl with Birds and Branches, 2000

4 x 15 x 8 in. (10.2 x 38.1 x 20.3 cm)
Hand-built white stoneware; hump mold; carved;
colored slip; glaze cone 6 oxidation
Photo by Jay York

I use strong, simple three-dimensional shapes as surfaces for bold graphic compositions. The images I use are derived from natural forms and everyday objects.

Suzanne Kraman
Bowl with Leaf and Vine Pattern, 2000

7 x 9 x 7 in. (17.8 x 22.9 x 17.8 cm)
Wheel thrown; carved; vitreous engobes; bisque cone
06; glaze cone 6 electric, oxidation

Matisse's wallpapered interior back-
drops were the inspiration for these
simple repetitive patterns that use
images and areas of texture.

Ronan Kyle Peterson
Beetle Berry Bowl, 2001

6 x 12 x 12 in. (15.2 x 30.5 x 30.5 cm)
Wheel-thrown and altered stoneware; added textured
slab; Tile 6 slip; sgraffito; cutouts; celadon glazes;
glaze cone 10 wood
Photo by Tom Mills

This is one of the first pots in which I started to feel that I might be glimpsing what my work as a ceramicist was going to be. I especially like the hidden space inside the enclosed vessel.

Kristin Doner
Large Pinchpot Bowl, 2001

6½ x 13 x 13 in.
(16.5 x 33 x 33 cm)
Pinchpot; glaze; engobe; bisque
cone 04 electric

Winthrop Byers
Blue and Green Fruit Bowl, 2002

2¾ x 10½ in. (7 x 26.7 cm)
Wheel-thrown stoneware; sprayed and layered glazes;
wood ash; bisque cone 07; cone 11 gas, reduction
Photo by Sandra Byers

I smooth the inside of my bowls with a rib so that they will be functional and leave throwing lines on the outside to show how they were created.

Joy Lappin
Ritual Bowl I (with Chinese Squares), 2001

5 x 14 in. (12.7 x 35.6 cm)
Wheel-thrown stoneware; carved; layered glazes of
lichens and red bronze; multi-fired; glaze cone 08 raku
Photo by Tony Deck

Ancient pottery and bronze vessels have always fascinated me. Their forms are timeless and affirm mankind's ongoing need to create. Through the application of various layers of glazes and multiple raku firings, my vessels are deliberately crusted to appear as if buried and aged for centuries.

Susan Farrar Parrish
Autumn in the Sun, 2002

14 x 16 x 17 in. (35.6 x 40.6 x 43.2 cm)
Slab built; carved; underglazes; clear glaze;
bisqued; glaze cone 5
Photo by Seth Tice-Lewis

Jennie Bireline
Tri-Pod Bowl, 1996

8 x 12 x 12 in. (20.3 x 30.5 x 30.5 cm)
Assembled from wheel-thrown and hand-built
earthenware elements; terra sigillata; single-fired
to cone 04; 23K gold leaf applied post firing
Photo by George Bireline

This bowl is intended for celebratory occasions rather than for everyday use. My work often references earlier cultures.

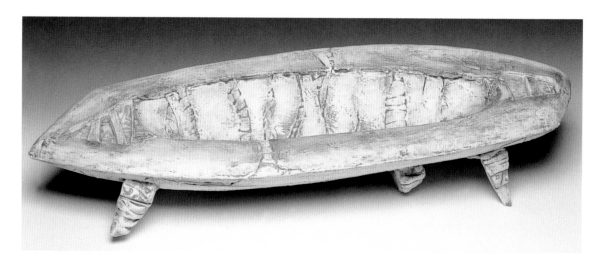

Karen Jennings
Explorer, 2000

35½ x 11¹³⁄₁₆ x 9¹³⁄₁₆ in. (90 x 30 x 25 cm)
Press-molded white grog stoneware; hand built; black
wattle; colored engobes; bisque cone 6

*My influences for form and color
are inspired by the waterways of
Sydney, Australia.*

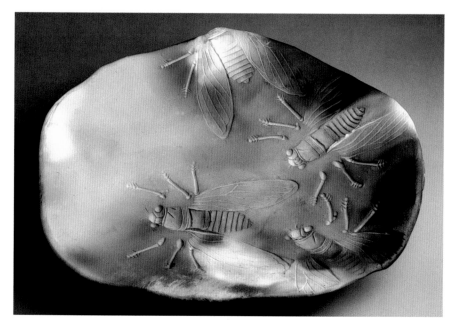

Pamela Wood
Untitled, 2001

5 x 20 x 17 in.
(12.7 x 50.8 x 43.2 cm)
Slab-built porcelain; sawdust

*These pieces are
slab constructed,
nature inspired,
and sawdust fired.*

Jane Perryman
Burnished Double-Walled Bowl, 2001

9 1/16 x 7 1/2 x 7 1/2 in. (23 x 19 x 19 cm)
Coiled porcelain mix; burnished porcelain slip; clay,
wax, paper resist; bisque 1760°F (960°C);
saggar fired, sawdust
Photo by Graham Murrell

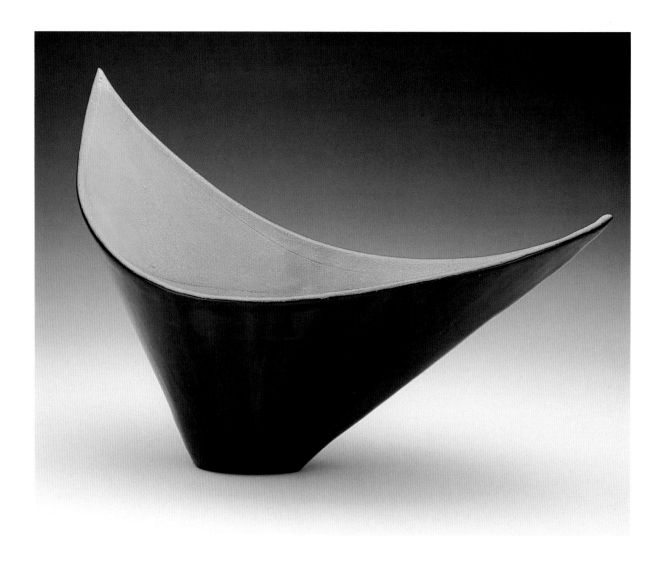

Tabbatha Henry
Nothing to Hide with Nothing Inside, 2001

8 x 12 x 6 in. (20.3 x 30.5 x 15.2 cm)
Slab-built terra cotta; glazed; glaze cone 04

Rachel Leitman
Two Bowls, 2001

7 x 7 x 4 in. (17.8 x 17.8 x 10.2 cm)
Slip-cast porcelain; glaze cone 10

Ravit Lazer
Untitled, 2000

7⅞ x 9¹³⁄₁₆ x 15¾ in. (20 x 25 x 40 cm)
Wheel-thrown and altered stoneware; glaze cone 6

Gale Golovan Rattner

Organic Red #4, 1998

4 x 13 in. (10.2 x 33 cm)
Hand-built porcelain; slab, coiled, carved, pierced;
multi-glazed; naturally occuring copper-red crackle;
bisque cone 04; glaze cone 9 reduction
Photo by John Bedessem

Don R. Davis

Slanted Bowl Group, 1999

14 x 14 x 13 in. (35.6 x 35.6 x 33 cm) (largest); 5 x
5 x 4½ in. (12.7 x 12.7 x 11.4 cm) (smallest)
Wheel-thrown porcelain; engobe and wax resist; glaze;
cone 7, light reduction
Photo by Tim Barnwell

Geoffrey Wheeler
Condiment Bowls, 2000

4 x 5 x 5 in. (10.2 x 12.7 x 12.7 cm)
Wheel-thrown and altered porcelain; slab-built spoons;
cones 6 and 04
Photo by Peter Lee

Leslie Thompson
Maori Border–Patterned Pueblo Bread-Raising Bowl, 2000

9 x 11 x 11 in. (22.9 x 27.9 x 27.9 cm)
Wheel thrown and carved; black interior glaze;
1800°F (982°C); 2300°F (1260°C)
Photo by Simon Chatwin

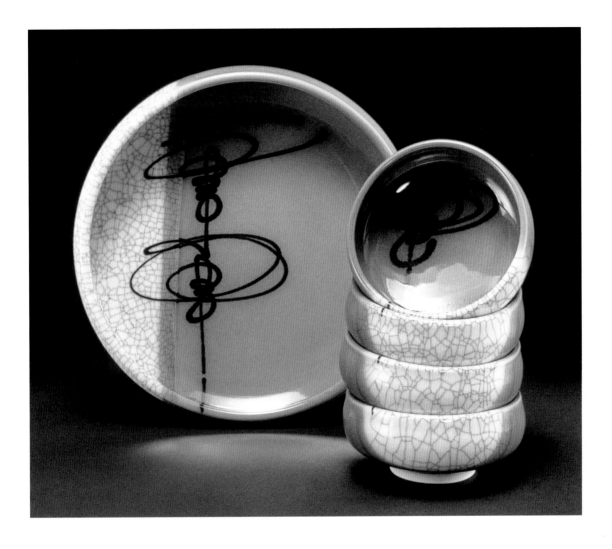

Deborah Shapiro

Salad Set, 2001

3 x 12½ x 12½ in. (7.6 x 31.8 x 31.8 cm) (large bowl)
Wheel-thrown grolleg porcelain; mint, crackle glazes;
chrome/tin "cranberry" flush; bisque cone 07;
glaze cone 10 oxidation
Photo by Courtney Frisse

Carol-Ann Michaelson
Untitled, 2000

4 x 10½ x 18 in. (10.2 x 26.7 x 45.7 cm)
Wheel-thrown and altered; hand-built additions; ash
glazes; bisque cone 06; cone 08 electric

*The river I live and work beside
has influenced the boat-form and
runny river ash glazes that
appear in my work.*

Mark Peters
Dimpled Bowl, 2002

3 x 9 x 9 in. (7.6 x 22.9 x 22.9 cm)
Wheel-thrown stoneware; soda/wood
Photo by artist

Jennifer Amy Yates
Soda Shell, 1998

4 x 13 in. (10.2 x 33 cm)
Slump-molded porcelain; soda cone 10, reduction
Photo by University of Wisconsin-Stout

I like to make pots that work well and look like the materials they are made of.

Shawn Ireland
Rectangle Server, 2000

15 x 8 x 3 in. (38.1 x 20.3 x 7.6 cm)
Slab-built stoneware; raw glazed; rope impressed;
glaze cone 10 wood
Photo by Walker Montgomery

Rich Conti
Serving Bowl, 2001

22 x 18 x 8 in. (55.9 x 45.7 x 20.3 cm)
Stoneware; tumble stacked; glaze cone 11 wood

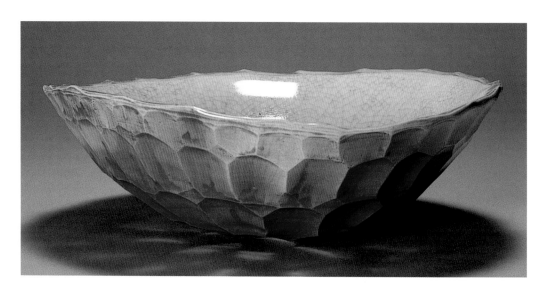

Tony Moore
Large Wood-Fired Shell Bowl, 2000

5 x 14 x 14 in. (12.7 x 35.6 x 35.6 cm)
Slab-built and wheel-thrown porcelainous stoneware;
carved; crackle shino; Avery slip; glaze cone 11+,
2372°F (1300°C) wood, fired for 24 hours
Collection of Graham and Pat Smith of Derby, England

The intimacy and directness of clay and the relationship of the human hand to the material, coupled with the organic nature of the wood-fired process, are what engage me.

Stephen Sell
Fluted Bowl, 2001

4 x 10 x 10 in. (10.2 x 25.4 x 25.4 cm)
Wheel-thrown and altered; shino glaze; bisque cone
05; glaze cone 10

Joseph Bruhin
Bowl, 1999

3 x 5 x 5 in. (7.6 x 12.7 x 12.7 cm)
Wheel-thrown stoneware; finger-wiped shino glaze;
glaze cone 11 wood

Jennifer Amy Yates

Seven Soups, 1999

Bottom: 15 x 8 x 4 in. (38.1 x 20.3 x 10.2 cm)
top: 15 x 5 x 2½ in. (38.1 x 12.7 x 6.4 cm)
Wheel-thrown and altered porcelain; soda cone 10
Photo by University of Wisconsin-Stout

Lori Nicolosi
Ice Cream Bowl, 2000

2½ x 6 x 6 in. (6.4 x 15.2 x 15.2 cm)
Slab- and coil-built white stoneware; applied
underglazes; clear glaze; cones 05 and 5
Photo by Charles Kline

Greg Daly
Set of Cut Tripod Bowls, 2001

17¾ x 6¼ in. (45 x 16 cm)
Wheel thrown; cut rim; tripod feet; 2372°F (1300°C) oxidation

Angela D. Rose
Untitled, 2001

9¾ x 9¾ x 5¼ in. (24.8 x 24.8 x 13.3 cm)
Wheel-thrown porcelain; oribe; salt cone 10 wood
Photo by artist

Paul Winspear

Purple Bowl, 2001

3 x 12 x 2½ in. (7.5 x 30.5 x 6.5 cm)
Wheel-thrown white stoneware; copper
and cobalt glaze; chun; red iron oxide;
cone 10, heavy reduction
Photo by Helen Mitchell

*Of all the things I make, bowls
excite me the most. I especially
like the way the clay slides
through my fingers as the bowl
takes its own wonderful shape.*

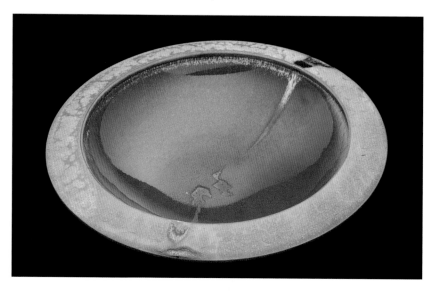

Mark Heimann

Krater, 2001

6 x 10 x 10 in. (15.2 x 25.4 x 25.4 cm)
Wheel-thrown porcelainous stoneware; coil, stamp
additions; high-temperature glazes; poured cobalt
interior; sprayed cobalt, copper exterior; bisque cone
04; glaze cone 10
Photo by Courtney Frisse

*A krater is an ancient
Greek vessel used to
mix wine and water. The
bowl usually had two
handles, to provide a
better grip.*

Lois Sharpe
Sea Bowl, 2001

Wheel-thrown and altered porcelain; rutile glaze;
crater glaze exterior; glaze cone 10 gas reduction
Photo by Marty Felding

The crater glaze was achieved
with silicon carbide slip and
multiple glazes brushed on.

John McCoy

Ice Cream Bowl, 2001

4 x 4½ x 4½ in. (10.2 x 11.4 x 11.4 cm)
Wheel-thrown porcelain; glaze cone 12 wood;
anagama kiln

James A. Coquia

Tea Bowl, 2001

4½ x 5 x 5 in. (11.4 x 12.7 x 12.7 cm)
Wheel thrown; shino; glaze cone 10
Photo by artist

Robert "Boomer" Moore
Bowl on Wheels, 2000

14 x 20 x 13 in. (35.6 x 50.8 x 33 cm)
Wheel thrown; assembled; altered; sprayed layers of high-
fire feldspathic glaze; bisque cone 020; glaze cone 10
wood, fired 18 hours; catenary cross-draft kiln

*My pieces are intended to
be playful, fun, whimsical,
and animated, but they are
still pots.*

Steve Schaeffer

"Chun" Bowl, 2001

7 x 8 x 6 in. (17.8 x 20.3 x 15.2 cm)
Porcelain; wax resist on black slip;
oil/salt cone 10 wood
Photo by artist

*My work is constantly developing; by open-
ing up the surface of the pot I open myself
to new ideas and exploration.*

95

Nesrin During
Shell Bowls, 2002

6¼ x 15¾ x 12½ in. (16 x 40 x 32 cm)
Coil-built German Westerwalder clay; ash-glazed interior;
glaze wood/salt 2336–2372°F (1280–1300°C)
Photo by Stephan During

Lee Akins
Tipped Bowl, 1985

11½ x 17½ in. (29.2 x 44.5 cm)
Coil-built terra cotta; textured; raw glaze; cone 01

Katie Love
Bowl, 2002

7 x 8½ x 8 in. (17.8 x 21.6 x 20.3 cm)
Wheel-thrown and slab-built porcelain;
soda cone 10, reduction

Joe Davis

Slip-Carved Bowl #3, 2000

3½ x 4 x 3 in. (8.9 x 10.2 x 7.6 cm)
Wheel-thrown white stoneware; slip carved; celadon
glazed; cone 10 gas, reduction

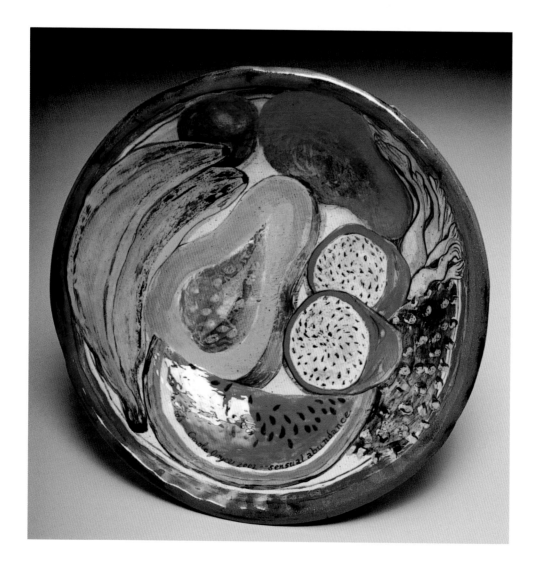

Carola Joyce
Sensual Abundance Bowl, 2002

3¼ x 13 in. (8.3 x 33 cm)
Slab-formed terra cotta; textured; iron oxide stain;
layered white slip; colored underglazes; clear interior
glaze; bisque cone 04; glaze cone 05
Photo by Michael Noa

I love images of abundance, freedom, and sensual pleasures, so that is what I paint.

Ron Korczynski
Nutty Sun, 2002

18 x 12 x 2 in. (45.7 x 30.5 x 5 cm)
Earthenware slab; hump molded; raised surface
areas; underglaze; glaze cone 04

Lea Zoltowski
Pinched Bowl, 2001

8¾ x 21 in. (22.2 x 53.3 cm)
Wheel-thrown and pinched
stoneware; assembled; zinc silicate crystalline glaze; cone 9
oxidation, controlled cooling
Photo by artist

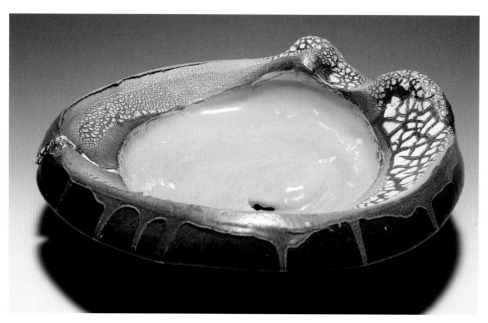

Jessica Wilson
Untitled, 1999

4 x 21 x 22 in. (10.2 x 53.3 x 55.9 cm)
Wheel-thrown stoneware; assembled; double fired cone 10, reduction

Janet Buskirk

Shallow Bowl, 1999

4 x 12 x 12 in. (10.2 x 30.5 x 30.5 cm)
Slab-built white stoneware; wheel-thrown foot;
deflocculated slip; glaze cone 10 gas
Photo by Bill Bachhuber

I made about 100 of these, and the slip peeled off 90 of them, but I kept making them because I like them.

Mark Peters
Six Sided Bowl, 2002

4 x 9 x 9 in. (10.2 x 22.9 x 22.9 cm)
Wheel-thrown stoneware; altered; wood/soda
Photo by artist

Dale Huffman
Bowl, 1998

5 x 21 x 21 in. (12.7 x 53.3 x 53.3 cm)
Wheel-thrown white stoneware; all natural ash glaze;
bisque cone 05; glaze cone 13 wood
Photo by Michael Ray

Hwang Jeng-Daw

Tea Bowl: Nature, 1998

3¹³⁄₁₆ x 5⅛ x 4¾ in. (10 x 13 x 12 cm)
Wheel-thrown and altered; natural wood-ash glaze;
cone 8 anagama, reduction

James A. Coquia
Knee Bowl, 2000

5 x 6¼ x 5 in. (12.7 x 15.9 x 12.7 cm)
Hand formed; unglazed; cone 13 wood
Photo by artist

Jeff Kise
Untitled, 2001

6 x 10 x 10 in. (15.2 x 25.4 x 25.4 cm)
Wheel thrown; burnished; low-fire interior glaze;
bisque cone 06; glaze cone 04;
glaze saggar fired cone 08
Photo by Tim Barnwell

Robert "Boomer" Moore

Come Along Bowl, 2001

10 x 12 x 8 in. (25.4 x 30.5 x 20.3 cm)
Wheel thrown; assembled; altered parts; sprayed
layers of high-fire copper-bearing glazes; sandblasted;
bisque cone 08; glaze 10 gas reduction

Gloria Young
Pedestal Bowl with Fruit and Flowers, 2000

17⁵⁄₁₆ x 16¹⁄₈ x 5⁷⁄₈ in. (44 x 41 x 15 cm)
Slab built; hand-painted majolica glaze; cone 04
Photo by Sal Criscillo

I like my work to have a playful element and often a dual purpose—using trompe l'oeil, or visual trickery, to create a work that is two-dimensional on one side, three-dimensional on the other, with space inside for real fruit or flowers. I'm inspired by urns and vases of antiquity, so I make pots to look like paintings of pots.

Matthew A. Yanachuk
Set of Bowls Square/Triangle/Oval, 2000

Oval: 3¾ x 10¼ x 9 in. (9.5 x 26 x 22.9 cm);
square: 5½ x 11 x 12½ in. (14 x 27.9 x 31.8 cm);
triangle: 5½ x 12 x 11 in. (14 x 30.5 x 27.9 cm)
Slip-cast white earthenware; wax-resist

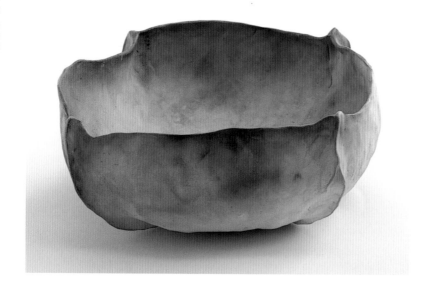

Mimi Bardagjy
4-Ribbed Bowl, 2001

4 x 8 x 8 in. (10.2 x 20.3 x 20.3 cm)
Pinched white clay; bisque cone 6; sawdust
fired with gold accents on ribs and rims
Photo by Paul Bardagjy

*This hand-built piece is inspired by
my love of the sea and sea shells.*

Karin M. Boudet
Dragonflies, 2002

$4\frac{1}{2}$ x 11 x 11 in. (11.4 x 27.9 x 27.9 cm)
Wheel-thrown stoneware; hand-built handle;
sprig-mold decoration; bisque cone 04;
glaze cone 6
Photo by Sir Kyle Garner

Kathi Roussel
Strange Fruit, 1999-2000

21 x 18 x 7 in. (53.3 x 45.7 x 17.8 cm)
Wheel-thrown stoneware; pedestal altered; forms
added; slip; shino glaze; carbon trap glaze;
glaze cone 10

Barbara Hanselman
Punch Bowl, 2001

6 x 12 x 12 in. (15.2 x 30.5 x 30.5 cm)
Hand built and pinched; hollow-handle cups;
weathered bronze and bamboo ash; bisque cone 05;
glaze cone 5 electric

Cindy Couling

El Sol, 2001

4 x 15 x 3 in. (10.2 x 38.1 x 7.6 cm)
Slab built; hand carved; colored slips; high-fire rutile
glaze; bisque cone 04; glaze cone 10
Photo by Lynn Hunton

*I reproduce images several ways
with different media, such as slip
carving and lino block carvings
printed on both clay and paper. I
like to see how much the image
changes as the medium changes.*

Carolyn Genders
Blue Silhouette-Square Bowl, 2001

10¼ x 11 x 11 in. (26 x 28 x 28 cm)
Coil-built white earthenware; painted vitreous slips;
wax resist, sgraffito; semi-matte transparent
interior glaze; cones 1/02
Photo by Mike Fearey

Bowls have an open, welcoming, expansive quality. They are optimistic, full of promise, whether full or empty, and, by their very nature, generous in form. Bowls are modest but surprising, only revealing themselves fully when the viewer peers into them. Bowls reflect my attitude to life.

Maggie Zerafa
Quatrefoil Bowl, 2001

5⅛ x 9 in. (13 x 23 cm)
Wheel-thrown; altered; shino glaze; cone 10 gas
Photo by Tom Baker

*The rusty reds of the highly
reduced shino glaze are perfect
for this autumn leaf design.*

Karen Newgard
Serving Bowls, 2002

8 x 12 x 7 in. (20.3 x 30.5 x 17.8 cm) (left);
7 x 10 x 6 in. (17.8 x 25.4 x 15.2 cm) (right)
Wheel thrown; terra sigilatta; sgrafitto;
liner glaze; salt cone 06

Judy Thompson

Bowl, 2001

6 x 11 x 5½ in. (15.2 x 27.9 x 14 cm)
Wheel-thrown porcelain; slip painting; sgraffito;
clear gloss glaze; cone 6 oxidation

Having begun my art career as a painter, I try to throw forms with elegant shapes that will act as blank canvases for painted decoration.

Kay Irish
Rabbits on the Run, 2001

4 x 9 x 9 in. (10.2 x 22.9 x 22.9 cm)
Wheel thrown; airbrushed; handpainted;
underglazes; bisque cone 06; glaze cone 6
Photo by Courtney Frisse

I've always been inspired by animals and nature. They both have found their way onto my pots.

I am an admirer of Chinese painting. In the brush paintings of the great masters, reverence for ordinary objects is expressed, whether it is a common flower or a bunch of vegetables on the kitchen table. Through the skillful simplicity of their brushwork, not only the likeness but also the spirit of the object is captured. My objective is to incorporate this essence into my pottery.

Maya Bohler
Sunflower Bowl, 2000

4 x 11 x 11 in. (10.2 x 27.9 x 27.9 cm)
Porcelain; majolica

Janice Strawder

Nesting Bowl Set, 1998

Largest: 8½ x 18 x 18 in. (21.6 x 45.7 x 45.7 cm)
Wheel-thrown earthenware; majolica;
bisque cone 05; glaze cone 04
Photo by artist

My work is inspired by the rhythms and patterns I observe in nature. The forms become successively smaller, the surface design has an underlying geometric base, and the color shifts came from mixing varying amounts of coloring stains on a palette.

Mark Johnson
Low Bowl, 2001

4 x 12 x 12 in. (10.2 x 30.5 x 30.5 cm)
Wheel-thrown and carved white stoneware; layered
glazes; soda cone 10
Photo by artist

Andrew P. Linton
Triangle Bowl, 2002

5 x 10½ x 10½ in. (12.7 x 26.7 x 26.7 cm)
Wheel-thrown stoneware; altered; carved;
glaze cone 09 reduction
Photo by Jim Kammer

Starting with a basic bowl form, I "pull" in the wall slightly and then roll (or fold) over the lip. This gives the bowl a more substantial, finished look. I then use a small loop tool to carve an "echo" of the stamped triangle indentations.

Steve Schaeffer
Nesting Bowls, 2001

7 x 8 x 6 in. (17.8 x 20.3 x 15.2 cm)
Porcelain; wax resist on black slip;
oil/salt cone 10 wood
Photo by artist

Kimberly Davy

Bowl, 2002

6⅛ x 4⅜ x 2 in. (15.5 x 11 x 5 cm)
Wheel-thrown porcelain; altered; spriggs with
polychrome glaze; glaze cone 6
Photo by artist

*As a ceramic artist who explores issues inherent to
wheel throwing and pottery traditions, I engage in two
processes. Focusing on form and style, I use the wheel
as a point of departure to create multiple parts, employ-
ing "cut and paste" to create form and clarify function.
In decorating, I apply color theory, referring to painting
and our natural environment to create mood. I am cap-
tivated by this process of transformation.*

Linda Forrest
Porcelain Bowl, 2001

3½ x 7⅛ in. (9 x 18 cm)
Wheel-thrown porcelain; cobalt inlaid
line; zinc slip; white semi-matte glaze;
single-fired cone 8 electric
Photo by Pam Ryan

Giles Le Corre
Blue Bowl, 2001

7 x 21 x 5 in. (17.8 x 53.3 x 12,7 cm)
Hand-thrown stoneware; white glaze;
layered glazes; cone 10 reduction
Photo by Chris Honeywell

I trail using brushes and apply a range of colored glazes in layers. When fired, the glazes melt and blend with each other, creating a rich fusion of colors.

Jill MacMillan

Constellation, 2001

4½ x 8½ x 4 in. (11.4 x 21.6 x 10.2 cm)
Wheel-thrown stoneware; cobalt glaze; rutile spray;
glaze cone 10 reduction
Photo by Bart Katsen

I spent about six months throwing just bowls. I was trying to see how thin, how wide, how precarious I could make a bowl but still have it well constructed and usable. This one of the best from that time.

Marcelle Klein
Three Bowls, 2001

4¾ x 4¾ in. (12 cm x 12 cm) each
Wheel-thrown stoneware; altered; glazed; cone 12 electric
Photo by Noa Streichman

The bowls begin as closed forms. Puncturing them releases the air inside and alters them, and that gives each piece its shape and character.

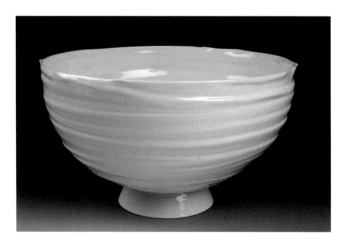

Sarah Tanner
Breeze Bowl, 2000

6¾ x 11¾ in. (17 x 30 cm)
Turned in plaster (on a lathe); molded in plaster; slip cast, semi-porcelain slip; bisque 2120°F (1160°C); glaze 2048°F (1120°C)
Photo by Steve Tanner

Living as I do overlooking the coastline, I witness a continuous communication between the land and sea. The washing in and out of the tides creates a rhythmic motion, and it is this fluidity of movement and the marks left by motion, such as when the tide flows are recorded in the sand, which led to the making of "Breeze Bowl." I try to capture traces of movement in the liquidity of plaster as it is spun wet around a central form. The pressure of my hands records an expression in the moments before the plaster sets.

Sandra Byers
Light Dancer, 2000

2⅜ x 2⅜ in. (6 x 6 cm)
Wheel-thrown and carved porcelain; lightly glazed;
bisque cone 04; cone 9½ electric, controlled cooling
Photo by artist

> The time-etched layers of a Yosemite rock face, the rhythmic ripples of a snowdrift, the undulating edges of torn white paper: a potter can allude to them all in one small white bowl.

Laura Jean McLaughlin
High Dive Act, 1998

8 x 8 x 3 in. (20.3 x 20.3 x 7.6 cm)
Slip-cast porcelain; black slip; sgraffito; low-fire
colored glazes; bisque cone 6; glaze cone 08
Photo by Lonnie Graham

*I derive most of my imagery
through a process much like the
surrealistic artists: I step out of
the here and now and allow the
imagery to pour out, without ever
second-guessing myself.*

Pam Arena
Bowl with a View, 2000

Slab-built white earthenware; velvet underglazes; choxil, underglaze crayons; wire; glaze cone 04 electric
Photo by Mike Noa

Inspired from a recent visit to Italy and the movie, A Room with a View, this bowl evokes images of cities and countryside, art museums, ancient ruins, and the passion embodied in everyday Italian life.

Barbara Hanselman
Ice Cream Bowl & Spoon on Pretzel Base, 2001

9 x 8 x 8 in. (22.9 x 20.3 x 20.3 cm)
Hand-built stoneware; pinched; coiled pretzels; slab-built and stretched
spoon; multi-glazed; bisque cone 06; glaze cone 5 electric

Sheldon Ganstrom
Arroyo Bowl, 2002

7 x 10 x 10 in. (17.8 x 25.4 x 25.4 cm)
Wheel thrown; glaze; engobe;
glaze cone 07 raku
Photo by artist

James R. Page, Jr.
Sacrificial Bowl, 2002

6 x 6½ x 6½ in. (15.2 x 16.5 x 16.5 cm)
Wheel thrown; carved and textured; low-fire
clear crackle raku glaze; bisque cone 08;
glaze cone 08
Photo by Sheldon Ganstrom

137

Mark Peters
Bowl with Textured Rim, 2002

3½ x 10 x 10 in. (8.9 x 25.4 x 25.4 cm)
Wheel-thrown stoneware; soda/wood
Photo by artist

Deborah J. Weinstein

Carved Bowl III, 2001

5 x 14 x 13½ in. (12.7 x 35.6 x 34.3 cm)
Slip-cast porcelain; carved; sprayed with celadon-like
glaze; single-fired cone 10
Photo by Kohler Design Studio Photography

*I think of this pattern
of carving as brain
coral and try to keep
a continuous flow of
line.*

139

Carol Selfridge
Richard Selfridge
Fleurs de Nuit Bowl, 2002

4 x 14 in. (10.2 x 35.6 cm)
Wheel-thrown terra cotta; majolica;
glaze cone 04
Photo by Richard Selfridge

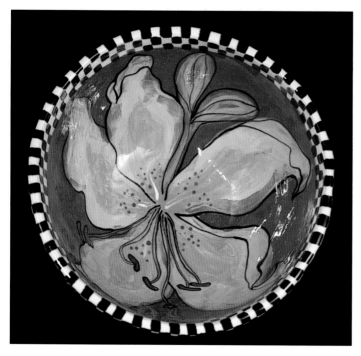

Linda J. Gleason
Lily, 2000

3½ x 6¾ x 3⅛ in. (8.9 x 17.2 x 7.9 cm)
Hand-built terra cotta; pinched; underglaze; clear
glaze; bisque cone 04; glaze cone 06
Photo by Debra Jones

*I often use living flowers of the
season—many from my garden—
as my inspiration.*

Viva Jones
Banana Bowl, 2002

5 x 7½ x 4 in. (12.7 x 19 x 10.2 cm)
Wheel-thrown; layered underglazes;
bisque cone 04; glaze cone 06
Photo by artist

Greg Daly
Resist Luster-Decorated Bowls, 1993

19⅞ in. (48 cm) diameter
Wheel thrown; porcelainous glaze; glaze resist and
sgraffito; resin luster from gold, bismuth, and zinc;
2372°F (1300°C); 1346°F (730°C) oxidation

Mary Cay

"In the End," from the Mushroom Series, 1999

8 x 12 x 12 in. (20.3 x 30.5 x 30.5 cm)
Wheel-thrown earthenware; hand-built, altered lip;
terra sigillata; underglaze; gold luster;
bisque cone 04; luster cone 022
Photo by Mad Dog Studio

Working with the theme of premature death, this piece presents the golden egg of birth, death, and the gift of the near-death experience.

Janet Lee Korakas
Cool Respite, 2000

$6^{11}/_{16}$ x 9 x $6^{5}/_{16}$ in. (17 x 23 x 16 cm)
Hand-built, press-molded, and sculpted stoneware;
glazes; bisque cone 06; glaze cone 9
Photo by Jeremy Dillon

Barbara Knutson

Lattice Bowl with Ginko Leaf, 2001

5 x 12 x 12 in. (12.7 x 30.5 x 30.5 cm)
Wheel-thrown white stoneware; extruded brown
stoneware; hump molded; pressed; cut;
glaze cone 10 reduction
Photo by Tim Barnwell

Mark Walnoch
Green Bowl, 2000

6 x 6¾ x 6¾ in. (15.2 x 17.1 x 17.1 cm)
Wheel thrown and altered; cryolite crater glaze;
cone 07; glaze cone 6

Sylvia Lampen
Untitled, 2002

5 x 8 x 5 in. (12.7 x 20.3 x 12.7 cm)
Coil-built red clay; Amaco glazes; bisque cone 04;
glaze cone 05
Photo by Michael Noa

Naomi Rieder
Vessel, 1999

6¾ x 9 x 9 in. (17.2 x 22.9 x 22.9 cm)
Hand-built white earthenware; burnished; layered terra sigillata; bisque
cone 08; pit fired

Julie Thompson
Strata Bowl, 2002

3 x 5 in. (7.6 x 12.7 cm)
Wheel-thrown and altered porcelain; colored porcelains stacked, cut and recombined; bisque cone 08;
glaze cone 6
Photo by artist

*Even after it's been fired, all the
flowing stripes and patches on
these bowls remind me of soft
porcelain as it's being thrown.*

Raphael Molina-Rodriguez
Tea Bowl with Maple Box, 2001

5 x 3½ x 3½ in. (12.7 x 8.9 x 8.9 cm)
Wheel-thrown stoneware; porcelain slip; shino liner;
soda cone 10

Stephen Heywood
Stacking Bowls, 2000

10 x 6 x 6 in. (25.4 x 15.2 x 15.2 cm)
Wheel-thrown stoneware; cone 10 wood
Photo by artist

Laura O'Donnell
Acrobat Tea Bowls, 2001

5 x 4 x 4 in. (12.7 x 10.2 x 10.2 cm)
Wheel-thrown earthenware; carved; modeled; yellow slip;
red iron oxide; glaze; bisque cone 08; glaze cone 02
Photo by Chris Berti

Collette L. Smith
Functional Wheel-Thrown Bowl, 2000

Wheel thrown; colored slips; cone 10, reduction

Cynthia Bringle
Bowl, 2000

12 x 12 in. (30.5 x 30.5 cm)
Wheel thrown and faceted; brushwork; cone 10
Photo by Tom Mills

Holly Walker
Untitled, 2000

9 x 9¼ x 9¼ in. (22.9 x 23.5 x 23.5 cm)
Pinched earthenware coils; single fired
cone 04
Photo by Tom Mills

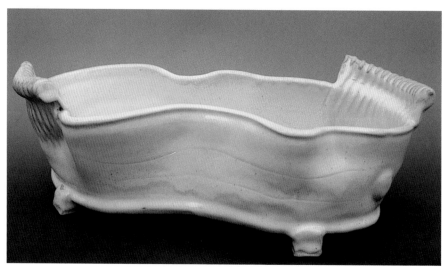

Jo-Ann Gartner
French Vanilla Cream, 2001

5 x 14 x 6¼ in. (12.7 x 35.6 x 15.9 cm)
Wheel-thrown and altered Miller 510 stoneware;
striated handles; bisque cone 06; cone 6
Photo by artist

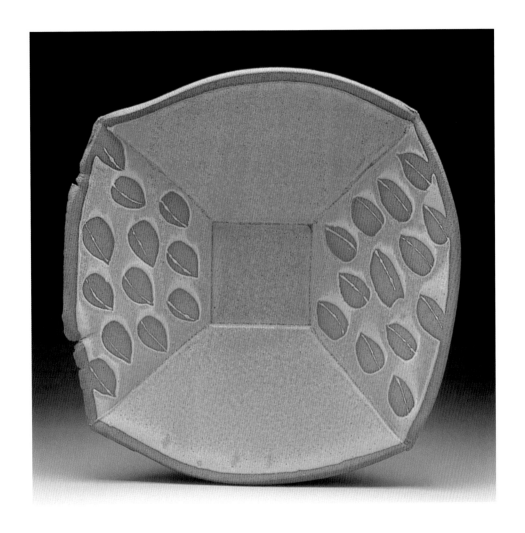

D. Hayne Bayless
Bowl with Leaf Resist Design, 2001

2 x 12 x 12 in. (5 x 30.5 x 30.5 cm)
Slab-built stoneware; copper matte glaze; resist;
cone 10, reduction
Photo by artist

Veronica Newman

Spiral Bowl, 2000

3 x 9½ in. (7.6 x 24.1 cm)
Hand-thrown translucent porcelain; cut; incised;
oxides; glaze cone 8 oxidation
Photo by Paul Adair

*Inspiration for my work comes from
sources as diverse as ancient
Mycenaean and Minoan pottery,
plants in the garden, and the views
of the ever-changing Scottish landscape as seen from my workshop.*

Victor Greenaway
Porcelain Spiral-Lipped Bowl, 2002

7½ x 13 in. (19 x 33 cm)
Wheel-thrown porcelain; altered; eggshell white glaze;
cone 8, reduction

Susan Beiner
Revereware Bowl, 1999

8 x 13 x 13 in. (20.3 x 33 x 33 cm)
Slip cast; assembled; multi-fired; cone 6;
glaze cone 018 luster

I have been influenced by the rich tradition established by European porcelain manufacturers of the 17th and 18th centuries.

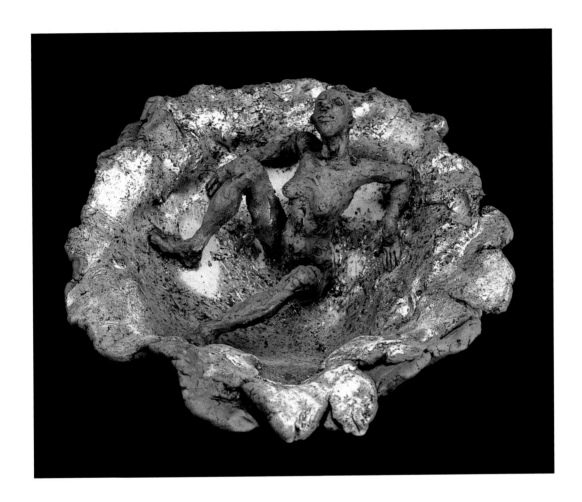

Sharon Bladholm

At Rest, 2000

9 x 15 x 16 in. (22.9 x 38.1 x 40.6 cm)
Hand- and slab-built stoneware; raku glazes;
cone 04 raku
Photo by Greg Woodward

Amy Lenharth
Pumpkin Bowl, 2000

10 x 12 x 10 in. (25.4 x 30.5 x 25.4 cm)
Wheel-thrown and altered stoneware;
cone 10 gas, reduction
Photo by Janet Ryan

*I try to capture the spirit of
nature by incorporating real leaf
impressions into my work. I am
inspired by the many shapes and
sizes of leaves.*

Cathi Jefferson
Redart Rectangle Bowl, 2001

10 x 9 x 11 in. (25.4 x 22.9 x 27.9 cm)
Wheel-thrown and altered porcelainous stoneware;
bottom added; salt/soda cone 10
Photo by John Sinal

Grace Pilato
Ian Stainton
Untitled, 1999

10 x 8 x 8 in. (25.4 x 20.3 x 20.3 cm)
Wheel thrown and hand carved; burnished black terra
sigilatta; raku reduction in sawdust chamber
Photo by John Sheckler

Marjory Kline
Notched Salad Bowl, 2001

4½ x 10 in. (11.4 x 25.4 cm)
Wheel-thrown stoneware; John Hesselberth and char-
coal satin matte glazes; bisque cone 06; glaze cone 6
Photo by D. James Dee

*In designing this salad bowl, I sought
to break the continuous line of the
rim by carving out notches that
would also serve as resting places
for two serving utensils.*

Lisa Eller Davis

Two = One, 2001

4 x 5½ in. (10.2 x 14 cm)
Wheel-thrown stoneware; trimmed; wax resist; underglaze, crackle glaze; bisque cone 06;
cone 06 raku

*Playing with optical illusions
captivates me. Thus the
double-lipped bowl, deliberately glazed to cause the
viewer to wonder if it's one
or two.*

Steve Irvine
Double-Walled Bowl with Gold Leaf, 2001

$3\frac{1}{4}$ x 11 x 11 in. (8 x 28 x 28 cm)
Double-walled press-molded stoneware; metallic glaze;
gold leaf; glaze cone 10 reduction

Ljubov Seidl
Silence of the Books, 2001

7½ x 13¾ in. (19 x 35 cm)
Wheel-thrown porcelainous stoneware; underglazes;
sgraffito; clear glaze; bisque cone 06;
glaze cone 5; gold cone 016
Photo by George Seidl

Vessels communicate with
us, and they can be used as
an artist's canvas to express
feelings or experiences. The
upright sides of bowls are
ideal for that.

Scott Place

Bowl Form, 2000

11 x 5 x 4 in. (27.9 x 12.7 x 10.2 cm)
Wheel-thrown and altered earthenware; glazes;
cone 04, oxidation

Sandra Benscoter

Memories and Maturity, 1996

9½ x 15 x 11 in. (24.1 x 38.1 x 27.9 cm);
8 x 21 x 9 in. (20.3 x 53.3 x 22.9 cm)
Wheel-thrown and altered stoneware; hand built; pink
engobes; translucent glaze; PVC pipe; faucet handle;
bisque cone 08; glaze cone 10 gas
Photo by Craig Phillips

This fun and functional work is part of my exploration into one's daily rituals. It's a small replica of a ball-and-clawfoot tub from my childhood. To my childish imagination, its hardware sometimes inspired me to imagine those parts taking other forms.

Bacia Edelman
Bowl, 1990

14 x 12½ x 4½ in. (35.6 x 31.8 x 11.4 cm)
Press-molded stoneware clay; underglazes; bisque
cone 04; glaze cones 05 and 06

Carolyn Genders
"Eclipse" Square Bowl, 2001

7¹⁄₁₆ x 14¼ x 14¼ in. (18 x 36 x 36 cm)
Coil-built white earthenware; painted vitreous slips;
wax resist; semi-matte transparent
interior glaze; cones 1/02
Photo by Mike Fearey

Cathryn Schroeder Hammond
Water (from 4 bowl series: "Earth, Air, Fire and Water"), 1999

3½ x 8 x 8 in. (8.9 x 20.3 x 20.3 cm)
Wheel-thrown and altered stoneware; poured
and sprayed glazes; bisque cone 06;
glaze soda cone 10
Photo by artist

I strive to produce work that is technically strong and well-crafted, and that I enjoy using and living with. Colors and shapes are inspired by the natural world around me—my gardens, the seashore, the woods, and mountains.

David Greenbaum
Mandala Bowl, 2001

6 x 23 in. (15.2 x 58.4 cm)
Wheel thrown; carved; burnished; saggar/pit fired
Photo by Randy Battista

Kent McLaughlin
Porcelain Bowl with Altered Rim, 2001

8 in. (20.3 cm) diameter
Porcelain; altered; layered glazes;
glaze cone 10 reduction
Photo by Tom Mills

Suze Lindsay
Pedestal Bowl, 1999

10 x 12 x 4½ in. (25.4 x 30.5 x 11.4 cm)
Wheel-thrown and altered stoneware; assembled;
slips; glazes; salt cone 10
Photo by Tom Mills

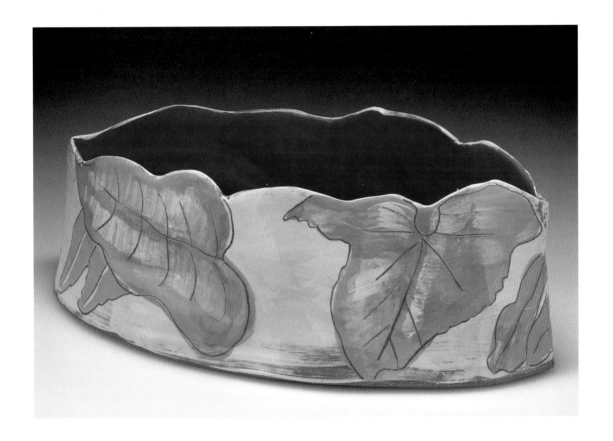

Susan Kowalczyk
Leaf Bowl (Green), 2000

5 x 13½ x 8 in. (12.7 x 34.3 x 20.3 cm)
Hand-built earthenware; slips; glaze; cone 03
Photo by Andrew Fortune

Bonnie Seeman
Yellow Bowl with Leaves, 2002

9 x 12 x 12 in. (22.9 x 30.5 x 30.5 cm)
Wheel-thrown and altered porcelain; hand built;
cone 10, oxidation
Photo by artist

Lynn Fisher

Bowl, 2002

6 x 8 in. (15.2 x 20.3 cm)
Slab-built stoneware; impressed leaf additions; fake
ash glaze; glaze cone 9-10, oxidation
Photo by Stephen Kostyshyn

*I've always loved trees in the woods.
I started out intending to be a
forester, but was waylaid by clay. It
was natural for me to start playing
with leaves pressed into clay and
assembling them into pots or adding
them as decoration to the design.*

Gabriele Hain

Bowl with Three Pierced Fields, 1994

$1\frac{1}{2}$ x 3 x 3 in. (3.7 x 7.7 x 7.7 cm)
Slip-cast Limoges porcelain; pierced and carved;
transparent glaze; gold paint; blue-stained porcelain;
bisque 1112°F (600°C); bisque cone 08, 1796°F
(980°C); glaze cone 7, 2246°F (1230°C);
gold cone 018, 1382°F (750°C)
Photo by Franz Linschinger

*I try the impossible at least three
times before I give up...*

Rae Dunn

Wonder, 2002

5 x 9 x 9 in. (12.7 x 22.9 x 22.9 cm)
Coil-built stoneware; oxide; engobe; glaze cone 06

*The incompleteness and imperfection
of my work is part of the story, like
the way the absence of something in
our lives can stir powerful feelings
and show us the way to wholeness.*

Elspeth Owen

Bowl, 1997

9½ x 11 x 11 in. (24.1 x 27.9 x 27.9 cm)
Pinched grogged clay; porcelain slip containing
cobalt, vanadium; burnished; glaze; open saggar fired
1832°F (1000°C)
Photo by Nicolette Hallet

*I don't know anyone else who makes
pinched pots on the scale that I do—from
¼ inch (6 mm) to 20 inches (50.8 cm) tall.*

Katie Love
Shino Bowl, 2002

7 x 7½ x 7½ in. (17.8 x 19 x 19 cm)
Wheel-thrown and slab-built stoneware; black slip;
shino glaze; cone 10, reduction
Photo by artist

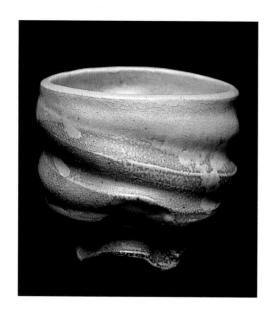

Lyn R. Woods
Diana's Bowl, 2000

4¼ x 4 x 4 in. (10.8 x 10.2 x 10.2 cm)
Wheel-thrown; altered; attached foot; bisque cone 08;
glaze salt cone 10
Photo by Diana Kersey

Richard Busch

Tea Bowl, 2002

2½ x 2⅜ x 2⅜ in. (6.4 x 6 x 6 cm)
Wheel-thrown stoneware; yellow celadon and
oribe glazes; wax-resist brush mark;
bisque cone 06; salt cone 11
Photo by artist

Robert Briscoe

Noodle Bowl, 2001

3½ x 6 x 6 in. (8.9 x 15.2 x 15.2 cm)
Wheel-thrown and paddled stoneware; colored and
combed slips; ash glaze; cone 9
Photo by Wayne Torborg

Susan Farrar Parrish
Cannas in the Sun, 2002

15 x 20 x 18 in. (38.1 x 50.8 x 45.7 cm)
Slab built; carved; underglazes; clear glaze;
bisqued; glaze cone 5
Photo by Seth Tice-Lewis

*My work reflects the natural environ-
ment that I see in my everyday life.*

Don R. Davis
Tripod Bowl, 1999

6 x 6 x 6 in. (15.2 x 15.2 x 15.2 cm)
Wheel-thrown and hand-built porcelain; wax resist;
sprayed oxides; glaze; cone 7, light reduction
Photo by Tim Barnwell

*Interiors are just as important
to me as exteriors.*

Jenny Lou Sherburne
Untitled, 1994

Wheel-thrown and pinched white earthenware; low-fire
glazes over textured surfaces; cones 04 and 06

Linda Arbuckle
Darted Bowl: Persephone, 2001

4 x 7 x 6 in. (10.2 x 17.8 x 15.2 cm)
Wheel-thrown terra cotta; darted; majolica;
glaze cone 03

Jo Forsyth
Rainbow Bowl, 2002

98½ x 137¾ in. (2.5 x 3.5 m)
Wheel-thrown terra cotta; slip; bisque cone 06;
glaze cone 02
Photo by artist

Lynn Smiser Bowers

Nested Soufflé Bowls, 2001

Largest: 4 x 12 x 12 in. (10.2 x 30.5 x 30.5 cm)
Wheel-thrown porcelain; stencils; wax resist; oxide;
glaze cone 10 reduction
Photo by E.G. Schempf

Ruchika Madan
Triple Dish, 2000

2½ x 22 x 8 in. (6.4 x 55.9 x 20.3 cm)
Hand-built white stoneware; hump mold; carved;
colored slip; cone 6, oxidation
Photo by Jay York

Randy Borchers
Pooka Ness
Butterfly Bowl, 2001

5½ x 6½ in. (14 x 16.5 cm)
Wheel-thrown stoneware; carved; incised; iron wash;
glazed; bisque cone 6; glaze cone 9
Photo by Peter Lee

Ryan J. Greenheck *left*
Basket, 2001

Wheel-thrown porcelain;
assembled; bisque cone 06;
soda cone 10

Tony Moore *below*
Large Wood-Fired
Stem Bowl, 2001

7½ x 16 x 16 in. (19 x
40.6 x 40.6 cm)
Slab-built and wheel-thrown
porcelainous stoneware; assembled; carved; incised; shino;
natural fly-ash glaze; glaze cone
11+, 2372°F (1300°C) wood,
fired for 24 hours
Collection of Graham and Pat
Smith of Derby, England

Kate Maury
Bowl, 2001

6 x 10 x 10 in. (15.2 x 25.4 x 25.4 cm)
Wheel-thrown porcelain; soda cone 10
Photo by Marty Springer and Bill Wikrent

Jerilyn Virden
Untitled (Double Walled Bowl), 2001

12 x 22 x 22 in. (30.5 x 55.9 x 55.9 cm)
Coil-built dark stoneware; slab built; Barnard-based
glaze; bisque cone 08; glaze cone 10
Photo by Harrison Evans

Virginia Scotchie
Pink Bowl, 2000

10 x 6 x 12 in. (25.4 x 15.2 x 30.5 cm)
Coil built; bronze, textured glazes;
glaze cone 6 oxidation
Photo by Brian Dressler

Ljubov Seidl
Sea World II Bowl, 2001

3¹⁵⁄₁₆ x 17¹¹⁄₁₆ x 13¾ in. (10 x 45 x 35 cm)
Wheel thrown and hand built; re-assembled; under-
glazes; clear glaze; bisque cone 06; glaze cone 5
Photo by George Seidl

*This line of bowls was
inspired by a 16th-century
Bernard Palissy work.*

Jenny Lou Sherburne
Serving Bowl, 1992

Wheel-thrown and altered earthenware; low-fire glazes
over textured, engobed surfaces; cone 06
Photo by Bobby Silverman

Jeff Hamilton
Krater, 2002

5½ x 6 x 6 in. (14 x 15.2 x 15.2 cm)
Wheel-thrown; glazed; bisque cone 07; glaze cone 05 raku
Photo by Evan Bracken

Although my firing technique is of ancient Japanese origin, my designs are inspired by the ancient art and mythology of Greece and medieval European sculpture.

Joy Lappin
Ritual Bowl II (Dragon Motif), 2001

4 x 12 in. (10.2 x 30.5 cm)
Wheel-thrown stoneware; carved; sprig molded; layered glazes of lichens and gold luster; multi-fired raku cone 08
Photo by Tony Deck

Lisa Eller Davis
Untitled, 2001

5 x 11 in. (12.7 x 27.9 cm)
Wheel-thrown raku; trimmed, cut foot, altered; wax
resist; copper sand glaze; bisque cone 06;
cone 06 raku
Photo by John Bonath

*The challenge of creating
visual movement on a solid
surface inspired these
glaze decorations.*

Andrew P. Linton
Divot Bowl, 2002

3 x 3½ x 3½ in. (7.6 x 8.9 x 8.9 cm)
Wheel-thrown orange stoneware;
altered; glaze; salt cone 10
Photo by Jim Kammer

*This small bowl is a variation
on the Japanese tea bowl.*

Aase Haugaard
Bowls, 2001

Left: 5⅛ x 5½ in. (13 x 14 cm);
right: 5⅛ x 6⅟₁₆ in. (13 x 15.5 cm)
Wheel thrown and altered; terra sigillata slip;
cone 10 wood

Terry Gess
Painted Bowl, 2001

8 x 13 x 13 in. (20.3 x 33 x 33 cm)
Wheel-thrown white stoneware; multiple slips

Douglass Rankin
Will Ruggles
Round Serving Dish , 2001

3½ x 12 in. (8.9 x 30.5 cm)
White stoneware slab; drape molded; wax resist;
brushed white slip; amber triangles; black finger dots
and salt cup wad marks; single fired salt/soda

Gary R. Ferguson
Carved Double-Walled Bowl. 2002

4 x 6½ x 6½ in. (10.2 x 16.5 x 16.5 cm)
Wheel thrown; hand built; carved; clear and copper raku
glazes; bisque cone 06; raku approximately cone 06

*Double-walled bowls are an
exciting shape to form and
decorate. The geometric
carved designs add some
stability to the dynamic raku
process.*

Linda Forrest

Porcelain Bowl, 2001

4⅛ x 5½ in. (10.5 cm x 14 cm)
Wheel-thrown porcelain; glazed; sgraffito;
cone 8 electric; luster 1472°F (800°C)
Photo by Pam Ryan

Hennie Meyer

Bowl on Feet, 2002

2³⁄₁₆ x 10⅝ x 10⅝ in. (5.5 x 27 x 27 cm)
Press-molded slab; underglaze; glaze; glaze 2048°F (1120°C)
Photo by artist

Betsy Begor Perkins

Trophy Bowl, 2001

5 x 9¼ x 9¼ in. (12.7 x 23.5 x 23.5 cm)
Marbleized stoneware; pieced slabs; porcelain slip;
clear glaze; beeswax finish; glaze cone 6, oxidation
Photo by Jeff Newcomer

Being catapulted into the dimension of creativity has been the most deeply satisfying thing I've ever experienced—and something I never imagined would happen to me. I took my first pottery class in 1994 at age 56. I never looked back. I love bowls; they represent comfort and hospitality to me.

Ricky Maldonado
Jack's Bowl, 2002

Coil-built terra cotta; slip; glaze dots; glaze cone 06
Photo by Image-Ination

Marilyn Dennis Palsha
"You Are What You Eat" Banana Bowl, 2002

3 x 16½ x 7½ in. (7.6 x 41.9 x 19 cm)
Slab-built red earthenware; wheel-thrown foot;
majolica; bisque cone 03; glaze cone 03
Photo by Seth Tice Lewis

This bowl is the latest example of a long-running theme of mine: women and desserts. It is inspired by an overexposure to women's magazines that alternate anorexic bathing-suit models with pages of dessert photographs.

Posey Bacopoulos
Oval Bowl, 2001

3 x 10½ x 7½ in. (7.6 x 26.7 x 19 cm)
Slab-built terra cotta on a hump mold;
majolica; stains; cone 04
Photo by Kevin Noble

Suzanne Kraman
Bowl with Leaves, 2000

7 x 9 x 7 in. (17.8 x 22.9 x 17.8 cm)
Wheel thrown; carved; vitreous engobes; bisque cone
06; glaze cone 6 electric, oxidation

Ben Carter
Wood-Fired Serving Bowl, 2001

6 x 8 x 6 in. (15.2 x 20.3 x 15.2 cm)
Wheel-thrown stoneware; incised lines on
surface; bisque cone 08; cone 10 wood
Photo by Chris Bledsoe

*I make serving bowls because I like
the relationships people form while
they are eating. I hope my bowls
lead to many great relationships.*

Lindy Shuttleworth
Swirl Bowl, 2001

3½ x 10 in. (8.9 x 25.4 cm)
Wheel-thrown stoneware; hollow rim; oribe;
glaze salt cone 10
Photo by Tom Mills

Una Mjurka
Carrot Bowl #3, 2002

4 x 11 x 11 in. (10.2 x 27.9 x 27.9 cm)
Hand built; layered engobes; oxide; glaze washes;
glaze multi-fired cones 06-04
Photo by artist

When viewing my work, one may consider an animal reference, while at the same time seeing the vessel reference. This way of seeing and thinking, the hybrid of sculpture and vessel, has always been interesting to me.

Marvin Sweet
Bowl and Stand, 2001

13 1/2 x 7 x 4 in. (34.3 x 17.8 x 10.2 cm)
Coiled; slab built; sandblasted; raku
Photo by David Powell

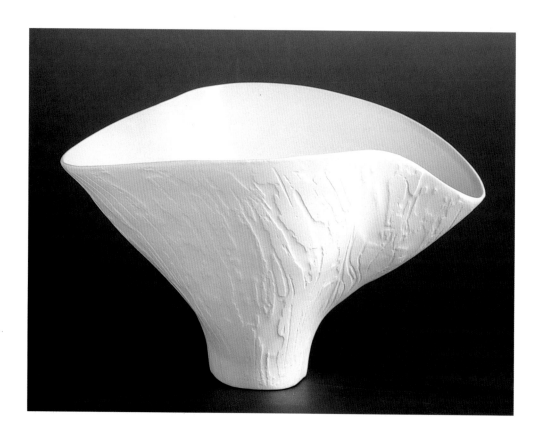

Norma Price
Snow Gum Bark, 2000

8 x 12¼ x 8¾ in. (20 x 31 x 22 cm)
Wheel-thrown and altered porcelain; terra sigillata,
glazed interior; cone 8 oxidation
Photo by Matt Kelso

Bryan Hiveley
Green/Orange Bowl, 2002

Coil built; layered low-fire glazes; cone 04

Catina Briscoe

Empty Bowl, 2001

22 x 13 in. (55.9 x 33 cm)
Wheel-thrown and coiled stoneware; carved; bisque
cone 08; glaze cone 6
Photo by Ted Dimond

*This piece was inspired by
Project Chili Supper, where
some of the proceeds went
to fight hunger.*

Lee Akins
Petal Bowl, 1986

7 x 18 x 18 in. (17.8 x 45.7 x 45.7 cm)
Coil-built terra cotta; underglazes; raw oxides; cone 01

Bonnie Baer
Untitled, 2001

4 x 9½ x 9½ in. (10.2 x 24.1 x 24.1 cm)
Leather-hard scraps of clay; textured;
interspersed with soft clay and
smoothed; oxides; underglaze; glaze
multi-fired cone 04/05
Photo by Michael Noa

Wolfgang Vegas
Recent Photography of the Land, 2001

$3^{13}/_{16}$ x $16^{13}/_{16}$ x $7^{7}/_{8}$ in. (10 x 43 x 20 cm)
Press molded; oxide; underglaze, glaze; luster;
cone 05 electric; luster cone 014
Photo by G. Boss

Cheryl Toth
Untitled, 2002

4 x 10 x 10 in. (10.2 x 25.4 x 25.4 cm)
Hump-molded stoneware; layered
glazes; cone 5
Photo by Bethany Poulin

Jane LeMaster
Woven Glory, 2001

3¼ x 14 in. (8.3 x 35.6 cm)
Coil-built white clay; Mason stains; clear
satin glaze; bisque cone 04; glaze cone 06

*Instead of using glazes to color the surface of
the clay, I mix the clay body with colored
stains and then use the colored clays to create my pieces.*

Connie Christensen
Untitled, 2002

13 in. (33 cm) diameter
Wheel-thrown porcelain; shino glazed; cone 10 reduction
Photo by John Bonath

Lea Zoltowski
Bowl, 2001

9¼ x 20½ in. (23.5 x 52.1 cm)
Wheel-thrown grolleg porcelain; assembled;
zinc silicate crystalline glaze; cone 9, oxidation,
controlled cooling
Photo by artist

Ginny Conrow

Pedestaled Bowl

7 x 9 x 7 in. (17.8 x 22.9 x 17.8 cm)
Porcelain; crystalline glaze cone 10
Photo by Roger Schreiber

I strive to make everyday functional ware that is beautiful to look at and delightful to use. I want movement and flow in my work.

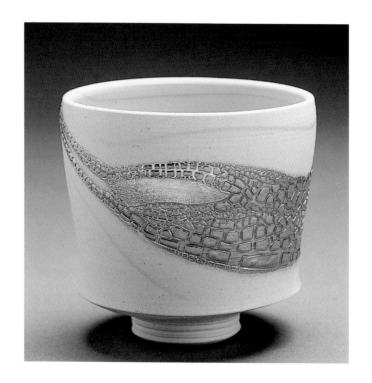

Lorenzo K. Nefulda
24 kt. Croc, 2001

4 x 4 x 3 in. (10.2 x 10.2 x 7.6 cm)
Wheel-thrown porcelain; glaze;
cone 10; gold luster
Photo by Brad Gioda

Catherine Dotson
Untitled, 2001

9 x 7½ in. (22.9 x 19 cm)
Wheel-thrown stoneware; altered;
salt cone 10; copper wire
Photo by Tom Mills

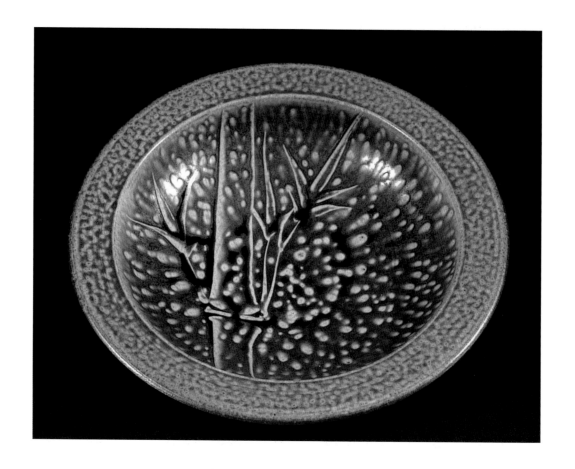

Richey Bellinger

Green Bowl

4 x 13 x 13 in. (10.2 x 33 x 33 cm)
Wheel-thrown porcelain; carved wax resist; wood ash
glaze; cone 10 reduction
Photo by artist

*I love the way the
glaze interacts with
the surface relief.*

Winthrop Byers

Magenta Fruit Bowl, 1998

3 x 13¼ in. (7.6 x 33.7 cm)
Wheel-thrown stoneware; sprayed and layered glazes;
bisque cone 07; wood ash cone 11 gas, reduction
Photo by Sandra Byers

Susan Rossiter

Three-Tiered Bowl, 1998

6 x 20 x 14½ in. (15.2 x 50.8 x 36.8 cm)
Stoneware; bamboo; cone 10, reduction
Photo by artist

Barbara Knutson
Lattice Bowl with Fish, 2001

6½ x 13 x 13 in. (16.5 x 33 x 33 cm)
Hand-built white stoneware; hump mold; pressed;
cut; extruded brown stoneware; bisque cone 06; glaze
cone 10, reduction
Photo by Tim Barnwell

While visiting an aquarium in Florida
I saw northern trout swimming in a
chilled tank against the current. I
loved the image and started putting
it on my pots.

Collette L. Smith
Functional Wheel-Thrown Bowl, 2001

Wheel thrown; colored slips; cone 10, reduction

Peggy Peak
Untitled, 2002

6 x 16 in. (15.2 x 40.6 cm)
Raku; copper matte and white and
yellow crackle glazes
Photo by artist

Therese O'Halloran
Raku Bowl, 2001

20 x 15 x 15 in. (50.8 x 38.1 x 38.1 cm)
Hand-built stoneware; raku
Photo by Ted Dimond

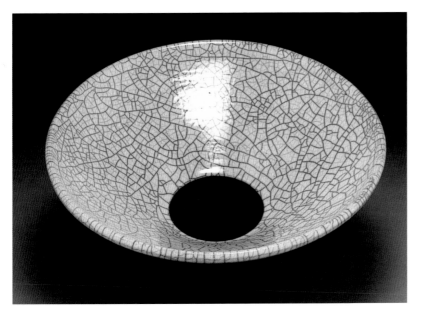

Sheldon Ganstrom
Anointing Bowl, 2002

7 x 10 x 10 in. (17.8 x 25.4 x 25.4 cm)
Wheel thrown; pulled base; raku glaze;
engobe; cone 07 raku

Angela Mellor
Sky Bowl, 1998

3⅛ x 4½ in. (8 x 11.4 cm)
Slip-cast bone china; latex resist; soluble salts;
glaze cone 7
Photo by Isamu Sawa

I am fascinated with the watercolor effects obtained by soluble colorants when applied to bare china without noticeably affecting the translucency. In fact, when lit from above it becomes more luminous and ephemeral.

Claire Verkoyen
Untitled, 2001

2¾ x 7½ in. (7 cm x 19 cm); 6¾ x 3¾ in. (17 cm x
9.5 cm); 3½ x 4¾ in. (9 cm x 12 cm)
Slip-cast translucent bone china; silkscreened
Photo by Jan van Esch

Laura Jean McLaughlin
Fish Bowl, 2001

14 x 14 x 4 in. (35.6 x 35.6 x 10.2 cm)
Slab-built white stoneware; slump molded; sgraffito;
slips; glaze; cone 8
Photo by Lonnie Graham

Karen Koblitz
My Obsession Series #2, 1998

8¾ x 14 x 14 in. (22.2 x 35.6 x 35.6 cm)
Wheel thrown, slab built, and pinched; underglaze;
glaze; bisque cone 04; glaze cone 06
Photo by Susan Einstein

This series blends historical references of high and decorative arts with 20th-century popular culture's interest in collectible objects.

Marcia Smith

Dreams, 2000

22 x 22 x 5 in. (55.9 x 55.9 x 12.7 cm)
Wheel-thrown and carved; splashed and applied texture;
sprayed underglaze, painted glazes, and pen-lettered
underglazes; bisque cone 04; glaze cone 7;
gold luster cone 018

*The surface treatment was
inspired by Dana Burnett's
poem, "Dreams."*

Chris Stanley
Double Skulls, 1999

Slip-cast porcelain; black, white engobe; hand
drawings; cut stencils; glaze cone 10
Photo by Eric R. Johnson
Courtesy of John Michael Kohler Art Center

Janette Loughrey
Banding Bowl, 2001

6 x 15¾ x 15¾ in. (15 x 40 x 40 cm)
Hand-built white earthenware; underglaze;
gold luster cone 02

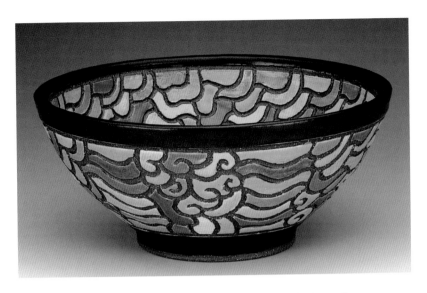

Norris Dalton
Deco Bowl, 1999

2⅝ x 6 x 2¼ in. (6.7 x 15.2 x 5.7 cm)
Wheel-thrown mid-range black clay;
sgraffito; cone 5
Photo by Michael Crow

The carved design is derived from an enduring interest in pre-Columbian art. My primary interest is color—especially the matte glaze shown here, which I have used for more than 30 years.

This bowl was inspired by a late night conversation with a friend that seemed to center on the changes our bodies go through as we age, but what's inside still feels the same—ageless.

Beth J. Tarkington
Metamorphosis Bowl, 2002

5 x 14 x 7½ in. (12.7 x 35.6 x 19 cm)
Slab and drape-molded red earthenware; carved; sculpted; layered slip; underglazes; oxides; multi-fired cone 05
Photo by Michael Noa

Richard Nickel
Alien Bowl, 2001

6 x 6 x 3 in. (15.2 x 15.2 x 7.6 cm)
Wheel-thrown earthenware; majolica; bisque cone 04;
glaze cone 04

Scott Lykens
Bowling for Batter, 2000

5 x 5 x 8 in. (12.7 x 12.7 x 20.3 cm)
Wheel-thrown hand-dug clay; altered; trimmed; slip;
layered glazes; bisque cone 07; glaze cone 3 gas

Brian Jensen
Untitled, 2002

3 x 4 x 4 in. (7.6 x 10.2 x 10.2 cm)
Stoneware and porcelain; soda
Photo by artist

Jason Bohmert

Tea Bowls, 2001

4 x 2½ x 2½ in. (10.2 x 6.4 x 6.4 cm)
Wet-faceted white stoneware; residual salt cone 11
Photo by artist

Julie Thompson
Carnival Bowl, 2001

2¾ x 5 x 5 in. (7 x 12.7 x 12.7 cm)
Ram-pressed porcelain with hand-built additions; slab
decorated; colored porcelains; bisque cone 08;
glaze cone 6
Photo by artist

Melissa Braden
Inguna Skuja
Marriage Dancers, 2000

11¼ x 11¼ x 3¼ in. (28 cm x 28 cm x 8 cm)
Slip-cast porcelain; sgraffito and stain; high-fire
glazes; 2336°F (1280°C)
Photo by Imants Kikulis

*By using a wide variety of colors
and textures juxtaposed against
bold line drawings, we create an
illusion of depth, more commonly
associated with paintings, on the
surface of our porcelain works.*

Housed together in a cup-board or on a shelf, tea bowls leave the group, perform their routines, and then reassemble to form a sculptural group in the cupboard.

Laura O'Donnell
Acrobat Tea Bowls, 2001

5 x 4 x 4 in. (12.7 x 10.2 x 10.2 cm)
Wheel-thrown earthenware; carved; modeled; yellow
slip; red iron oxide; glaze; bisque cone 08;
glaze cone 02
Photo by Chris Berti

Lynn Fisher
Bowl, 2001

10 x 9 in. (25.4 x 22.9 cm)
Slab-built stoneware constructed from cutout clay
leaves; fake ash glaze; glaze cone 9-10, oxidation
Photo by Stephen Kostyshynt

Susan Farrar Parrish
Hosta in the Sun, 2002

11 x 12½ x 12½ in. (27.9 x 31.8 x 31.8 cm)
Slab-built; carved; underglazes; clear glaze;
bisqued; cone 5
Photo by Seth Tice-Lewis

243

Naomi Rieder

Vessel, 1999

6¾ x 10 x 10 in. (17.2 x 25.4 x 25.4 cm)
Hand-built white earthenware; burnished; layered
terra sigillata; bisque cone 08; pit fired

Bob Nicholson

Horsehair 1, 2001

6 x 8 in. (15.2 x 20.3 cm)
Wheel-thrown Laguna B-Mix;
burnished; horsehair; raku
Photo by Lynn Hunton

*Hand burnishing with a
smooth stone compresses the
clay, creating a stronger pot
with a high surface sheen,
and carbon trapping from
burning horsehair creates
fascinating patterns.*

Lee Hazelgrove
Gathering Bowl, 1998

14 x 24 in. (35.6 x 61 cm)
Wheel-thrown white stoneware; found vines; clay
beads; sawdust/pine needles/straw; cone 04 pit
Photo by Dixon Withers-Julian

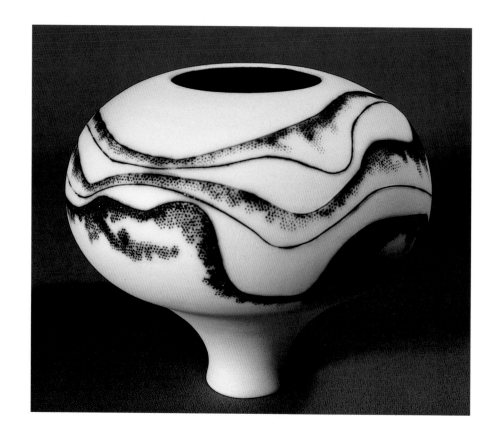

Bacia Edelman
Raised Bowl, 1987

9 x 10 x 10 in. (22.9 x 25.4 x 25.4 cm)
Wheel-thrown porcelain; (lower part thrown onto an
upside-down bowl); incised; glazed; black copper
oxide; sponged; bisqued; cone 9 oxidation

Hilary Scudder
Landline III, 2001

2 x 2¾ x 2¾ in. (5 x 7 x 7 cm)
Press-molded Buff stoneware; folded; copper oxide;
underglaze; cone 04, glaze cone 05
Photo by artist

Clay lives longer than we do.

Anne Bray
Pit-Fired Porcelain Bowl, 2001

3⅛ x 8¼ x 2¾ in. (8 x 21 x 7 cm)
Wheel-thrown porcelain; burnished; white terra sigillata slip;
beeswax wash; polish; no glazes; bisque 1832°F (1000°C);
smoked in outside garden pit with organic material

This effect was inspired by Ray Rogers's workshop in the UK, and it can only be obtained by using organic materials in an outdoor firing.

Lee Middleman
Celadon Textured Bowl, 2001

4 x 10 x 10 in. (10.2 x 25.4 x 25.4 cm)
Wheel-thrown white stoneware; textured;
expanded; bisque cone 06; glaze cone 10

This bowl experiments with texture, patterns, and the interplay between order and randomness. It was created to be functional, but also to intrigue the eye.

Ruchika Madan
Three Greek Vases, 2000

2½ x 5½ x 8 in. (6.4 x 14 x 20.3 cm)
Hand-built white stoneware; hump mold; carved;
colored slip; cone 6 oxidation

Barbara Knutson
Oval Pedestal Bowl with Handles, 2001

9 x 7 x 16 in. (22.9 x 17.8 x 40.6 cm)
Slab-built white stoneware; hollow handles; pressed;
rolled dots; bisque cone 06; glaze cone 10 reduction
Photo by Tim Barnwell

Steve Irvine
Press Mold Bowl with Gold Leaf, 2001

3¾ x 11¾ x 11¾ in. (9 x 30 x 30 cm)
Press-molded stoneware; cobalt blue glaze; gold leaf;
cone 10 reduction

Lee Middleman

Textured Bowl, 2001

4 x 10 x 10 in. (10.2 x 25.4 x 25.4 cm)
Wheel-thrown stoneware; textured; expanded; bisque
cone 06; glaze cone 10

*This bowl experiments with texture,
patterns, and the interplay between
order and randomness. It was created
to be functional, but also to intrigue
the eye and demand to be touched.*

Juan Granados
Spring Salad Bowl, 2001

Wheel-thrown and altered porcelain; bisque cone 08;
cone 10 electric, reduction
Photo by artist

Richard Baxter
Rolling Wave, 2001

3⅜ x 6½ in. (8.5 cm x 16.5 cm)
Wheel-thrown earthenware; cut; re-assembled; bisque
1760°F (960°C); glaze 1965°F (1074°C), oxidation
Photo by artist

This piece aims to put a real sense of movement back into a static piece. The "freeze frame" photographs of Muybridge have been an influence, as well as my studio location by the waters of the river Thames.

Jane Perryman
Burnished Smoke Fired Bowl, 2000

6¾ x 15¾ x 15¾ in. (17 x 40 x 40 cm)
Coiled porcelain mix; porcelain slip; burnished; clay,
wax, paper resist; bisque 1760°F (960°C);
sawdust smoke fired
Photo by Graham Murrell

*My work combines the influence
of traditional ethnic pottery from
India and Africa with a contempo-
rary interpretation.*

Marta Matray Gloviczki

Leaf Bowl, 2001

4 x 11 x 10 in.
(10.2 x 27.9 x 25.4 cm)
Hand-built porcelain; pressed
leaf and shell marks;
soda cone 10
Photo by Peter Lee

Rachel A. Euting

Embellished Bowl, 2001

3½ x 8¾ in. (8.9 x 22.2 cm)
Wheel-thrown porcelain; stamped;
wax resist; overglaze; bisque cone 06;
glaze cone 10
Photo by Janet Ryan

*I am very serious about
creating simple forms
that lend themselves as
a canvas for decoration.*

Holly Walker
Untitled, 2000

5 x 9½ x 9½ in. (12.7 x 24.1 x 24.1 cm)
Pinched earthenware coils; single fired
cone 04
Photo by Tom Mills

Sheila M. Lambert
Small Passions, 2002

$3\frac{1}{2}$ x 5 x 5 in. (8.9 x 12.7 x 12.7 cm)
Wheel-thrown and carved stoneware; layered high-fire
glazes; bisque cone 04; glaze cone 10 gas, reduction
Photo by Steve Mann

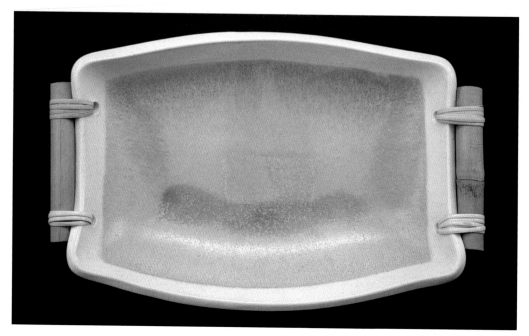

Cheryl Wolff
Serving Bowl with Bamboo Handles, 2001

3 x 9 x 12 in. (7.6 x 22.9 x 30.5 cm)
Slab-built white stoneware; layered glaze; wax resist; bisque cone 06; glaze cone 10, oxidation
Photo by Ken Weidner

Katie Love
Bowl, 2002

8½ x 9 x 8½ in. (21.6 x 22.9 x 21.6 cm)
Wheel-thrown and slab-built porcelain;
soda cone 10, reduction

Michael Kline
Triphid Bowl, 2000

5 x 12 x 12 in. (12.7 x 30.5 x 30.5 cm)
Thrown; altered; hand-built; underglaze painting;
yellow ochre glaze; salt; cone 10
Photo by Tom Mills

Suzanne Marie Cowan
Porcelain Bowl with Blushed Interior, 2001

4½ x 11½ in. (11.4 x 29.2 cm)
Wheel-thrown porcelain; albany black glaze exterior; black
slip interior; clear glaze; cone 10, reduction

Ben Carter
Wood-Fired Soup Bowl, 2001

4 x 5 x 4 in. (10.2 x 12.7 x 10.2 cm)
Wheel-thrown porcelain; porcelain slip; bisque cone
08; cone 10 wood
Photo by Chris Bledsoe

*This pot was inspired by my
love for soup.*

Diana Pittis
Untitled, 2001

4½ x 9 x 11 in. (11.4 x 22.9 x 27.9 cm)
Wheel-thrown and altered white stoneware; texture;
sprayed and layered glazes; cone 10, oxidation

Wesley L. Smith
Red Bowl, 2001

5 x 8 x 8 in. (12.7 x 20.3 x 20.3 cm)
Wheel-thrown stoneware; copper red formulas;
cones 08 and 10/11

Hodaka Hasebe

Bowl, 2001

5 x 9 x 9 in. (12.7 x 22.9 x 22.9 cm)
Wheel-thrown and altered; glazed; cone 10

Stephen Heywood

Tea Bowl, 2001

4 x 4 x 4 in. (10.2 x 10.2 x 10.2 cm)
Wheel-thrown stoneware; cone 10 wood
Photo by artist

Joe Davis

Slip-Carved Bowl #1, 2001

3 x 5¾ x 5¾ in. (7.6 x 14.6 x 14.6 cm)
Wheel-thrown white stoneware; slip carved; glazed;
salt/oil cone 11 wood

Randy Edmonson

Tea Bowl, 1999

3¾ x 5 x 5 in. (9.5 x 12.7 x 12.7 cm)
Wheel-thrown Shigaraki stoneware; incised; feldspar
inclusions; glaze cone 10-12; anagama kiln
Photo by Taylor Dabney

Randy Edmonson
Bowl with Spout, 2001

4 ½ x 7 x 7 in. (11.4 x 17.8 x 17.8 cm)
Wheel-thrown stoneware; incised; feldspar inclusions; salt cone 10
Photo by Taylor Dabney

Gayle Bair
Spiral Nesting Bowls, 2001

5½ x 8½ x 5 in. (14 x 21.6 x 12.7 cm)
Wheel-thrown porcelain; carved; slip (red
and black oxides and burnt umber); faux
celadon; transparent, clear glazes; bisque
cone 06; glaze cone 6 electric
Photo by artist

*My work is constantly evolving,
often taking risks to achieve that
one piece that "sings." In doing
so I also wind up with duds, but
even the duds have a purpose:
they become garden art.*

Carole Ann Fer
Batter Bowl, 2002

4¾ x 8 x 8 in. (12.1 x 20.3 x 20.3 cm)
Wheel-thrown porcelain; sgraffito; copper slip inlay;
semi-matte glaze; copper slip; bisque cone 08; glaze
cone 6 oxidation
Photo by Ken Woisard

Ben Krupka
Bowl, 2002

6 x 10 x 10 in. (15.2 x 25.4 x 25.4 cm)
Wheel-thrown porcelain; natural ash glaze; wood fired

Ginny Conrow
Oval Bowl

4 x 6 in. (10.2 x 15.2 cm)
Porcelain; crystalline glaze cone 10
Photo by Roger Schreiber

Connie Christensen
Untitled, 2001

12 in. (30.5 cm) diameter
Wheel-thrown porcelain; shino glazed;
cone 10 reduction
Photo by John Bonath

Stacey Letsch
Apple Bowl, 2001

8½ x 18 x 18 in. (21.6 x 45.7 x 45.7 cm)
Slab built; press molded; low-fired stains
Photo by Sheldon Ganstrom

Robert "Boomer" Moore
Potato Bowl on Wheels, 2000

12 x 20 x 12 in. (30.5 x 50.8 x 30.5 cm)
Wheel thrown; assembled; altered parts; sprayed layers
of high-fire, copper-bearing glazes; sandblasted; bisque
cone 08; glaze cone 10 gas, reduction

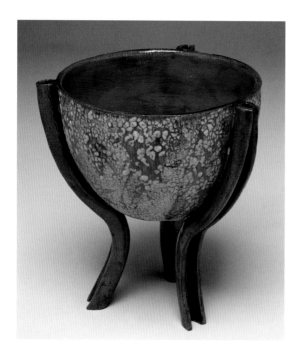

Cindy Watson
2001

10 x 8 x 8 in. (25.4 x 20.3 x 20.3 cm)
Slab-built terra cotta; oxide; slip; underglazes; lizard
glaze; bisque cone 04; glaze cone 05
Photo by Michael Noa

Scott Dooley
Industrial Kyli, 2002

10 x 10 x 10 in. (25.4 x 25.4 x 25.4 cm)
Hand-built porcelain; textured; oxide glaze;
cone 5 electric

Lynne McCarthy

Hang On, 2001

7 x 12 x 12 in. (17.8 x 30.5 x 30.5 cm)
Humped slab earthenware; textured; slips; oxides;
stains; glaze inside; bisque cone 04; glaze cone 05
Photo by Michael Noa

*I like working with texture and con-
trast—in this piece the contrast of
a smooth shiny inside and a highly
textured outside covered with slips.*

Daniel Rosen
Desert Moon, 2001

6 x 17 x 17 in. (15.2 x 43.2 x 43.2 cm)
Wheel-thrown; "eggshell" and "shiny
black" glazes; cone 10

For me, what separates ceramic arts from other media is the transfer of energy from the potter to the vessel, an exchange which I truly believe in and hold dear in my work. It is always my hope in my own creations that my audience will want to touch my work and feel the intangible.

Jason Bohmert
Serving Bowl, 2001

7 x 14 x 14 in. (17.8 x 35.6 x 35.6 cm)
Wheel-thrown white stoneware; 6 Tile and black slip brushwork; cone 11 wood
Photo by artist

Scott K. Roberts

Serving Bowl, 2001

2¾ x 10½ x 2½ in. (7 x 26.7 x 6.4 cm)
Kickwheel-thrown stoneware; altered; salt glazed with
slips and brush; single-fired cone 10
Photo by Rafael Molina

McKenzie Smith *above*

Bowl, 2001

13 x 13 x 8 in. (33 x 33 x 20.3 cm)
Stoneware; soda cone 10
Photo by artist

Jessica Dubin *left*

Flame Stitch Bowl, 2002

5½ x 8 x 8 in. (14 x 20.3 x 20.3 cm)
Wheel-thrown stoneware; oatmeal ash glaze; iron
oxide; bisque cone 06; glaze cone 10 reduction
Photo by Howard Goodman

*My work is driven by the desire to discover
and express the essence of that which is
common or everyday. The objects that I
make are rooted in the tradition of use,
and, as such, depend upon that realm for
their meaning and value.*

Emily Pearlman

Oval Bowl, 2001

$4\frac{1}{2}$ x 10 x $6\frac{1}{2}$ in. (11.4 x 25.4 x 16.5 cm)
Wheel-thrown stoneware; altered; cut; shaved;
trimmed; foot, handles added; carved; bisque cone
06; glaze cone 6 electric
Photo by James Dee

When I first started making pots, I wanted them to be as smooth, round, and symmetrical as possible. More recently, I have come to appreciate the potential of clay to be pushed, pulled, thrown, coiled, rolled, faceted, stretched, cut, textured, and assembled into any form, any shape, defined only by my skill and imagination. It is a never-ending source of interest and challenge.

Priscilla Hollingsworth
Wheat Meander Bowl (Yellow), 2002

7 x 10 x 10 in. (17.8 x 25.4 x 25.4 cm)
Hand-built terra cotta; double walled; applied decora-
tion; underglaze and oxide glaze; cone 04 oxidation
Photo by artist

*I have a recurring interest in rounded,
bulbous forms. I am also fascinated with
repetitive decoration that is poised some-
where between the natural world and
obsession.*

Shane M. Keena
Tidepool Bowl, 2002

7¼ x 22 x 22 in. (18.4 x 55.9 x 55.9 cm)
Slab-built stoneware; hump molded; wheel-thrown;
textured; Barnard clay stain; rutile spray; bisque cone
06; glaze cone 10 reduction
Photo by David Calicchio

Ben Krupka
4 Bowls, 2002

6 x 8 x 8 in.
(15.2 x 20.3 x 20.3 cm)
Wheel-thrown porcelain;
natural ash glaze;
wood fired

Douglass Rankin
Will Ruggles
Two Soup Bowls, 2001

3½ x 6½ in. (8.9 x 16.5 cm)
Wheel-thrown white stoneware; hump molded; cut feet; slip; single fired salt/soda cone 9 wood
Photo by Will Ruggles

Jon Arsenault *right*

Celadon Bowls, 2001

5 x 7 x 7 in. (12.7 x 17.8 x 17.8 cm)
Wheel-thrown porcelain; trailed porcelain slip; cone 10
Photo by artist

Mandy Wolpert *below*

Three Carved Porcelain Bowls, 2000/2001

2 to 2¾ x 4⅛ to 4¾ in. (5 to 7 x 10.5 to 12 cm)
Wheel-thrown porcelain; turned, chattered; carved;
copper red glaze; 2336°F (1280°C) reduction
Photo by Ian Hobbs

Linda Schusterman
Bowl with Tropical Pattern, 2001

4 x 20 in. (10.2 x 50.8 cm)
Wheel-thrown porcelain; incised; polychrome slips;
slip trailed; glaze cone 10 gas oxidation
Photo by John Woodin

My work is inspired by my travels to the Caribbean and Mexico. The lush vegetation and brilliant color and light found there influence my color choices and patterns.

Matthew A. Yanachuk
Flare Striped Bowl, 2001

5½ x 14 in. (14 x 35.6 cm)
Slip-cast white earthenware; wax-resist

Missy M. McCormick
Hatched Serving Bowl, 2001

6 x 10 x 10 in. (15.2 x 25.4 x 25.4 cm)
Wheel-thrown and altered stoneware; carved; flashing slip;
majolica; bisque cone 06; soda cone 11 cross-draft kiln

The enjoyment of monumental form, sturdy architecture, and ideas revolving around containment led me to explore the vastness and beauty of the bowl.

William Buhler

Wood Ash Bowl, 2001

2½ x 14 in. (6.4 x 35.6 cm)
Wheel-thrown white stoneware;
wood ash; bisque cone 08;
glaze cone 10 reduction
Photo by Maddog Studio

Rich Conti

Shallow Bowl, 1998

5 x 12 x 12 in. (12.7 x 30.5 x 30.5 cm)
Stoneware; tumble stacked; cone 11 wood

287

Molly Forman
Untitled, 2000

7 x 9½ in. (17.8 x 24.1 cm)
Wheel-thrown stoneware; colored slips;
salt cone 10

Gerbi Tsesarskaia
The Desert Bowl, 2001

5 x 11 x 11 in.
(12.7 x 27.9 x 27.9 cm)
Wheel-thrown stoneware;
cone 10 gas reduction
Photo by artist

Jeff Kise
Untitled, 2001

6 x 10 x 10 in. (15.2 x 25.4 x 25.4 cm)
Wheel thrown; burnished; low-fire interior glaze;
bisque cone 06; glaze cone 04; glaze saggar fired
cone 08
Photo by Tim Barnwell

Marilyn Richeda
Bowl with Striped Handles, 2000

4 x 16 x 12 in. (10.2 x 40.6 x 30.5 cm)
Wheel-thrown red earthenware; layered glazes;
multi-fired cone 04 gas
Photo by Smith-Baer, Ltd.

Harriet E. Ross
Untitled, 1999

6 x 8 x 5 in. (15.2 x 20.3 x 12.7 cm)
Wheel thrown; cone 10 reduction
Photo by James Dee

Carol Selfridge
Richard Selfridge
Raven Tea Bowl for Owen, 1998

3 x 5 in. (7.6 x 12.7 cm)
Wheel-thrown helmer stoneware; feldspathic stones;
rubber stencil; flashing slip; cone 12 wood
Photo by Richard Selfridge

James A. Coquia
Tea Bowl, 2000

3½ x 5½ x 5½ in. (8.9 x 14 x 14 cm)
Wheel thrown; feldspathic glaze with high percentage
of sodium carbonate as flux; cone 10
Photo by artist

Brian Jensen
Untitled, 2002

5 x 5 x 5 in. (12.7 x 12.7 x 12.7 cm)
Stoneware and porcelain; soda
Photo by artist

Stephen Mickey
Anagama-Fired Tea Bowl, 2002

4 x 14 x 4 in. (10.2 x 35.6 x 10.2 cm)
Stoneware; shino slip; copper red interior; anagama fired

D. Hayne Bayless
Bowl with Leaf Resist Design, 2001

2 x 12 x 12 in. (5 x 30.5 x 30.5 cm)
Slab-built stoneware; copper matte glaze; resist;
cone 10, reduction
Photo by artist

Sharon Shen

Sea Waves, 2000

6 x 9 x 6 in. (15.2 x 22.9 x 15.2 cm)
Wheel-thrown stoneware; carved; engobes;
bisque cone 8; salt cone 10
Photo by Jan Seale

*Sea Waves is an homage to Chinese
design and my love of the sea.*

295

Geoffrey Wheeler
Oval Bowl with Leaves, 1999

7 x 25 x 14 in. (17.8 x 63.5 x 35.6 cm)
Wheel-thrown and altered porcelain; cones 6 and 04
Photo by Peter Lee

Lucy Breslin
Summer Song #14, 2002

10 x 15 x 11 in. (25.4 x
38.1 x 27.9 cm)
Wheel-thrown white earth-
enware; hand built; lay-
ered glazes; bisque cone
07; glaze cone 04
Photo by Mark Johnson

Shannon Nelson
Dessert Bowl, 2000

5³⁄₄ x 7¹⁄₂ x 4 in. (14.6 x 19 x 10.2 cm)
Wheel-thrown white stoneware; altered; molded; hand
built; slip trailing; cone 6 oxidation
Photo by John Knaub

Jon Ellenbogen
Rebecca Plummer
Mixing Bowl Set, 1996

Largest: 14 in. (35.6 cm) diameter
Wheel-thrown and altered stoneware; cone 10;
reduction

Marc Verbruggen
Conversation Between Bowls, 2000

$^{13}/_{16}$ x $^{13}/_{16}$ in. (2 x 2 cm)
Wheel-thrown white stoneware; slips; salt 2336°F (1280°C) gas
Photo by Hans Vuylsteke

Deborah Shapiro
Crackle Bowl, 1998

1½ x 14 x 14 in. (3.8 x 35.6 x 35.6 cm)
Wheel-thrown grolleg porcelain; crackle glaze; slate
blue glaze accent; black overlaid glaze; bisque cone
07; glaze cone 10 oxidation
Photo by Kathryn Opp

*I love throwing low, wide serving
bowls. They become the canvas
for my dancing gestural designs.*

Gale Golovan Rattner
Organic Blues #10, 1999

7 x 15¼ in. (17.8 x 38.7 cm)
Hand-built porcelain; slab; coiled; carved; pierced;
multi-glazed; bisque cone 04; cone 8 reduction;
texture glaze cone 2 oxidation
Photo by Jerry Hoos

*As an artist and cancer survivor, I am
inspired by cell biology. The abstract organic
edge and textured glaze of this bowl suggest
cellular growth and activity as viewed
through a microscope. Pathology slides are
often stained blue. This vessel is often inter-
preted as water, wave, marine-life, and coral.*

Karl Knudson

Ash Glaze Bowl, 2001

5 x 12 x 12 in. (12.7 x 30.5 x 30.5 cm)
Wheel-thrown stoneware; multiple sprayed matte,
wood ash glazes; cone 10 reduction

Geoffrey Swindell

Bowl, 2002

2½ x 4¾ in. (6.4 x 12.1 cm)
Wheel-thrown porcelain; slip cast; incised; cone 7
Photo by Tom Swindell

*My bowls are inspired by my interest
in seashells, tin plate toys, and eroded
objects. I hope to create an object that
visually suggests a synthesis of these
varied source materials.*

301

Meredith Brickell

Oval with Canopy, 2001

3½ x 18 x 18 in. (8.9 x 45.7 x 45.7 cm)
Hand-built porcelain; matte glaze; cone 9 oxidation
Photo by Tom Mills

Neville French

Helmet Bowl and Vessel, 2001

Left: 4¾ x 4¾ x 4 in. (12 x 12 x 10 cm);
right: 3½ x 6¼ x 5½ in. (9 x 16 x 14 cm)
Wheel-thrown and altered; layered glazes;
multi-fired cone 11,
2282°F (1250°C)
Photo by Terence Bogue

I try to distill the essence of purity and evoke notions of quietude and transcendence through the expressive use of colored glaze and its relation-ship to form, tactility, space, and light.

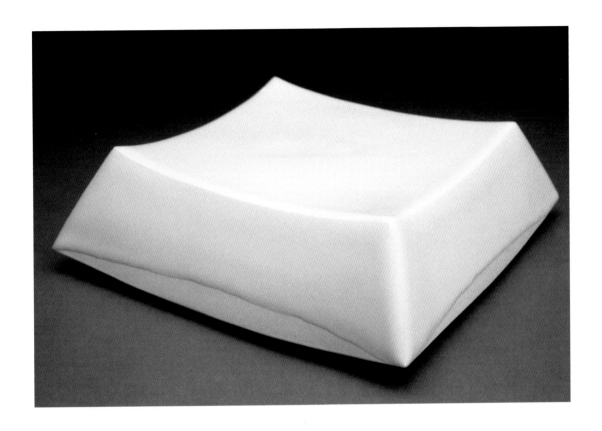

Rachel Leitman
Shallow Bowl, 2001

9 x 9 x 3 in. (22.9 x 22.9 x 7.6 cm)
Slip-cast porcelain; cone 10

Susan Rossiter
Two-Tiered Bowl, 1998

Larger: 6½ x 15 x 15 in. (16.5 x 38.1 x 38.1 cm)
Stoneware; bamboo; wax resist; rutile;
cone 10, reduction
Photo by artist

Marty Fielding

Untitled, 2002

5 x 15 x 15 in. (12.7 x 38.1 x 38.1 cm)
Wheel-thrown stoneware; layered glazes; wax resist;
cone 11 gas, reduction
Photo by artist

*Interior space is an important aspect
of a bowl, so I try to accentuate it while
throwing the bowl. Added decoration
further reveals its volume.*

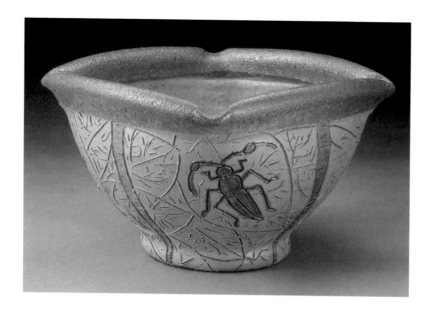

Ronan Kyle Peterson
Golden Beetle Bowl, 2001

6 x 8 x 8 in. (15.2 x 20.3 x 20.3 cm)
Wheel-thrown and altered stoneware; titanium slip; sgraffito; single-fired salt cone 10
Photo by Tom Mills

One of the few once-fired, salt-glazed pots that I am pleased with. I especially like the golden hue of the flashing slip and the almost-hidden leaf carvings.

Steven Glass
Bowl, 2001

7 x 12 x 12 in. (17.8 x 30.5 x 30.5 cm)
Wheel-thrown white stoneware; polychrome slip; underglaze; clear glaze; cone 7 oxidation
Photo by Mike Pocklington

Suze Lindsay
Ikebana Bowl, 2000

4 x 10 x 3 in. (10.2 x 25.4 x 7.6 cm)
Wheel-thrown and altered stoneware; assembled; pad-
dled; slips; glazes; salt cone 10
Photo by Tom Mills

Leslie Thompson
Hatched Triangles, 2001

6 x 11 x 11 in.
(15.2 x 27.9 x 27.9 cm)
Wheel thrown and carved;
black interior glaze; 1800°F
(982°C); 2300°F (1260°C)
Photo by Simon Chatwin

Jenny Browne
Carved Slipped Bowl, 1999

2³⁄₈ x 10¹⁄₄ x 10¹⁄₄ in. (6 x 26 x 26 cm)
Wheel-thrown stoneware; carved; blue slip; white
semi-opaque glaze; 2300°F (1260°C) oxidation
Photo by Michael Browne

*I use a thick layer of colored slip so that
when I carve away the background I
achieve a raised design.*

Theresa Yondo

Small Bowl Atop Three Plates, 2001

Bowl: 1 x 3½ x 3½ in. (2.5 x 8.9 x 8.9 cm)
Wheel-thrown porcelain; sgraffito; wax resist; glaze
cone 10 electric
Photo by Daniel Milner

This functional and decorative work is playfully designed to mix, match, and stack together, thus creating unfolding visual imagery.

Linda Arbuckle
Square Bowl: Falling Down, 2001

6½ x 6½ in. (16.5 x 16.5 cm)
Terra cotta; majolica; cone 03
Photo by Randy Battista/Media Image Photography

Naoko Gomi
Bubbly Turtles, 2002

2½ x 9 x 8 in. (6.4 x 22.9 x 20.3 cm)
Slab-built with colored porcelain; cone 9 oxidation

The bowl has no bottom. It will sway and the turtles will swim. The turtle is the symbol of eternal youth and longevity in Asia.

Scott Lykens
June Bug Bourbon Bowls, 2000

Left: 4 x 4 x 4 in.
(10.2 x 10.2 x 10.2 cm);
right: 4 x 3 x 3 in.
(10.2 x 7.6 x 7.6 cm)
Wheel-thrown, hand-dug brick clay;
trimmed; slips; glazed; overglazed;
cone 3 gas
Photo by artist

Makoto Hatori
Bowls in Sets of Five ("Ireko"), 2001

Smallest: 2 x 7 x 7 in. (5.5 x 17.7 x 17.7 cm);
largest: 3¼ x 12⅓ x 12⅓ in. (8.5 x 31.3 x 31.3 cm)
Wheel-thrown stoneware; salt-water sprayed interior;
black slip exterior; bottom upward when stacking kiln;
2282°F (1250°C) wood, oxidation; eight days in
Japanese bank kiln

*Five is a lucky number for
the Japanese.*

Lori Nicolosi
Life Spirals On, 2002

6 x 12 x 11½ in. (15.2 x 30.5 x 29.2 cm)
Slab- and coil-built stoneware; iron oxide; homemade
glaze called "straw"; bisque cone 05; glaze cone 5
Photo by Charles Kline

Nesrin During
Shell Bowls, 2001

4¾ x 10 ¼ in. (12.5 x 26 cm)
Coil-built German Westerwalder clay; wood/salt 2336–2372°F (1280–1300°C)
Photo by Stephan During

Cindy Watson
Untitled, 2001

5 x 7 x 7 in. (12.7 x 17.8 x 17.8 cm)
Slump-molded terra cotta slab; modeled; black copper
oxides; slip; glaze; bisque cone 04; glaze cone 05
Photo by Michael Noa

Tabbatha Henry

Swoosh, 2001

7 x 11½ x 7½ in. (17.8 x 29.2 x 19 cm)
Slab-built terra cotta; textured; layered underglaze
and glazes; cone 04
Photo by Tom Young

Since most of my work is sculptural, it tends to be monochromatic. I have started making bowl forms that allow me to explore color and texture more freely. I love the resulting tension that exists between the inside and outside—rough vs. smooth; shiny vs. matte, etc.

315

Ben Krupka
Batter Bowl, 2002

9 x 14 x 14 in. (22.9 x 35.6 x 35.6 cm)
Wheel-thrown porcelain; natural ash glaze; wood fired

Scott K. Roberts
Soup Bowl, 2001

3½ x 6½ x 3 in. (8.9 x 16.5 x 7.6 cm)
Kickwheel-thrown stoneware; salt glazed; slips; single-fired cone 10
Photo by Rafael Molina

My bowls, dishes, and way of working are richly influenced by the medieval potters and pottery of Southeast Asia.

Connor Burns
Small Bowl, 2000

3 x 4 x 4 in. (7.6 x 10.2 x 10.2 cm)
Wheel thrown; trimmed; single-fired
cone 10 gas, reduction
Photo by Al Surratt

*My work is made for
use, for daily joy.*

Blaine Avery
Carbon-Trapped Shino Bowl, 2001

7 x 9 x 9 in. (17.8 x 22.9 x 22.9 cm)
Carbon-trapping glaze; slip trailed;
cone 10 gas
Photo by Laura Avery

*My ideas are influenced by Southern
traditional folk pottery. The glazes and
slip-trailing I incorporate reflect my
interest in the timeless forms and decorations of the Southern folk potters.*

Janet Lee Korakas
Rococo Bowl, 1999

8¼ x 9½ x 6¹¹⁄₁₆ in.
(21 x 24 x 17 cm)
Hand-built, press-molded, and
sculpted stoneware; glazes; bisque
cone 06; glaze cone 8
Photo by Jeremy Dillon

Diana Pittis
Untitled, 2001

3½ x 8 x 11 in. (8.9 x
20.3 x 27.9 cm)
Wheel-thrown and altered
white stoneware; textured;
shino glaze; sprayed
celadon; cone 10 Geil
cartload downdraft kiln
reduction

Susan B. Goldstein
Raku Bowl, 2000

15 x 20 x 15 in. (38.1 x 50.8 x 38.1 cm)
Draped and hand-textured slab; raku fired
Photo by Jeff Rogers

Melissa Braden
Inguna Skuja
Housewives' Bowl with Stand, 2000

11¼ x 12 x 12 in. (28 cm x 30 cm x 30 cm)
Slip-cast altered porcelain; sgraffito; high-fire and low-fire glazes; salts 2336°F (1280°C); gold luster
Photo by Raimo Lielbriedis

Carolyn Genders
Crystal Bowl, 2000

3¹⁵⁄₁₆ x 11⅞ x 1⅞ in. (10 x 30 x 30 cm)
Coil-built white earthenware; painted vitreous slips; wax resist;
semi-matte transparent glaze; cones 1/02
Photo by Mike Fearey

Betsy Begor Perkins
Flared Bowl, 2001

4¼ x 8½ x 8½ in. (10.8 x 21.6 x 21.6 cm)
Marbleized stoneware; pieced slabs; porcelain slip;
clear glaze; beeswax finish; cone 6 oxidation
Photo by Jeff Newcomer

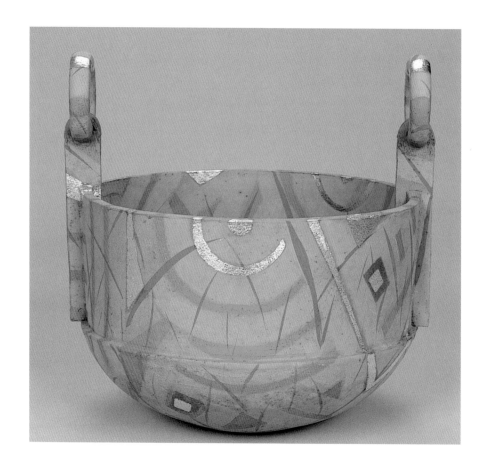

Jennie Bireline
Ring Handle Bowl, 2001

13 x 14 x 14 in. (33 x 35.6 x 35.6 cm)
Wheel-thrown and hand-built earthenware;
terra sigillata; single-fired cone 04;
23K gold leaf
Photo by Michael Zirkle

Virginia Scotchie

Avocado Knob Bowl, 2000

8 x 7 x 20 in. (20.3 x 17.8 x 50.8 cm)
Coil built; bronze, textured glazes; cone 6 oxidation
Photo by Brian Dressler

In my work I find inspiration from ordinary, everyday objects which I then abstract, dissect, and piece together.

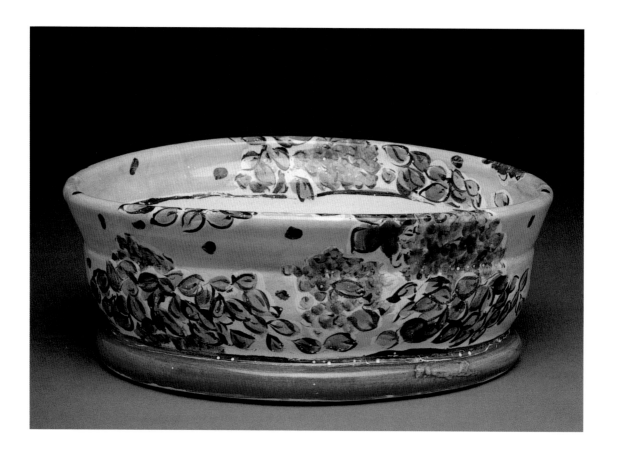

Joyce Nagata
Lilacs, 1997

8 x 14 x 8 in. (20.3 x 35.6 x 20.3 cm)
Wheel-thrown and altered terra-cotta earthenware;
majolica; bisque cone 04
Photo by John Carlano

Gloria Young
Still Life with Glass Bowl, 1998

15⅝ x 14⁹⁄₁₆ x 5½ in. (39 x 37 x 14 cm)
Slab built; hand-painted majolica glaze;
bisque cone 01; glaze cone 04
Photo by Stephen La Plant

Mark Walnoch
Untitled Bowl, 2000

10 x 8½ x 8½ in. (25.4 x 21.6 x 21.6 cm)
Wheel thrown and altered; colored slip; cryolite
crater and texture glazes; bisque cone 07;
glaze cone 6

Makoto Hatori
Bizen "Youhen" Teabowl, 2001

3⅝ x 6⅛ x 5⅛ in. (9.2 x 15.5 x 12.9 cm)
Wheel-thrown Bizen stoneware; natural wood/ash
glaze; 2336°F (1280°C) wood, reduction;
ten days in Japanese bank kiln

Lis Ehrenreich
White Bowl, 2000

$7^7/_8$ x $12^9/_{16}$ in. (20 x 32 cm)
Wheel-thrown red Danish earthenware; stamped;
engobe decorated; bisque 1472°F (800°C);
ash/borax glaze; 2156°F (1180°C) electric, reduction
Photo by Erik Balle Povlsen

Robert Briscoe
Noodle Bowl, 2001

$3^1/_2$ x $6^1/_4$ x 6 in. (8.9 x 15.9 x 15.2 cm)
Wheel-thrown and paddled stoneware; ash glazed
over colored slip; cone 9
Photo by Wayne Torborg

Gary Holt
Porcelain Bowl with Soluble Salts, 1999

8¼ x 6¾ in. (20.9 x 17.1 cm)
Wheel-thrown porcelain; soluble salt colorants;
multi-fired cone 06
Photo by Richard Sargent

Sandra Byers
White Carved Bowl, 1999

1¾ x 3¼ in. (4.4 x 8.3 cm)
Wheel-thrown and carved porcelain; lightly glazed;
bisque cone 04; cone 9½ electric, controlled cooling
Photo by artist

*I love the way porcelain
bowls catch the light and
thus spring to life.*

Bonnie Baer
Untitled, 2001

$5\frac{1}{2}$ x $6\frac{1}{2}$ x $6\frac{1}{2}$ in. (14 x 16.5 x 16.5 cm)
Slab built; textured with found objects; underglaze;
oxides; multi-fired cone 04/05
Photo by Michael Noa

Chito Kuroda
Day or Night? Bowl, 2002

$2\frac{3}{4}$ x $7\frac{1}{8}$ in. (7 x 18 cm)
Wheel-thrown white earthenware; slip;
underglaze; glaze
Photo by Miura Junko

*My work is simple and modern
wheel-thrown tableware.*

Shannon Nelson

Fanciful Bowl, 1999

3½ x 5 x 5 in. (8.9 x 12.7 x 12.7 cm)
Wheel-thrown white stoneware; altered; hand built;
glaze cone 6; gold luster accents cone 022, oxidation
Photo by John Knaub

Karen Newgard
Octopus Bowl, 2001

5 x 14 x 4 in. (12.7 x 35.6 x 10.2 cm)
Porcelain; terra sigilatta; sgrafitto; salt cone 10; gold
luster cone 020

Harriet Campe
Leaf Bowl #11, 2002

5 x 5 x 5 in. (12.7 x 12.7 x 12.7 cm)
Wheel-thrown porcelain; blue slip applied to bowl;
clear glaze; bisque cone 08; glaze cone 10 electric
Photo by Petronella Ytsma

I had the wonderful good fortune to grow up on a farm in southern Minnesota, where I spent many happy childhood hours making mudpies. Excellent preparation for a potter.

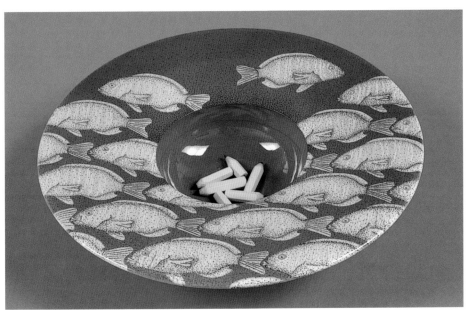

Stephen Patt
School, 1988

3 x 15 in. (7.6 x 38.1 cm)
Wheel-thrown porcelain; hand-built pencils; masked and airbrushed; stippled
underglaze and underglaze pencil; clear glaze; bisque cone 5; glaze cones 05-06
Photo by Susan Patt

Gina Freuen
Slab Foot Bowl, 2000

15 x 12 x 12 in. (38.1 x 30.5 x 30.5 cm)
Wheel-thrown porcelainous stoneware; slab built; textured; stains; clear glaze; bisque cone 04;
cone 6 gas, reduction
Photo by Hamilton Photography

Julie Sewell
Untitled, 2001

6½ x 4½ in. (16.5 x 11.4 cm)
Wheel-thrown stoneware; black gloss glaze; cone 6
Photo by Michael Noa

Meira Mathison
Untitled, 2001

12 x 10 x 7 in. (30.5 x 25.4 x 17.8 cm)
Wheel-thrown and altered; multi-layered glazes; ash
sprinkled; cone 10 reduction
Photo by Janet Dwyer

I love the whole idea of a basket. It
can serve food, hold valuables,
display flowers, or reflect the
beauty of its complex design.

Jill J. Burns
Flower Container, 2002

14 x 11 x 11 in. (35.6 x 27.9 x 27.9 cm)
Wheel thrown; assembled; cone 9 oxidation

Amy Lenharth
Pumpkin Bowl, 2000

10 x 12 x 10 in. (25.4 x 30.5 x 25.4 cm)
Wheel-thrown and altered stoneware;
cone 10 gas, reduction
Photo by Janet Ryan

Nature is my inspiration. I use real leaves to make impressions in the clay. I then incorporate these leaves into functional pots.

Mark Heimann
Five Golden Rings, 1999

8½ x 17½ x 17½ in. (21.6 x 44.5 x 44.5 cm)
Wheel-thrown white stoneware; hand-built additions; carved additions; sprayed high-
temperature ash, spodumene glazes; gold paint; bisque cone 04; glaze cone 10
Photo by Courtney Frisse

Gale Golovan Rattner
Organic Bronze Lava #4, 2002

4¼ x 10 in. (10.8 x 25.4 cm)
Hand-built porcelain; slab; coiled; carved; pierced;
multi-glazed; bisque cone 04; glaze cone 8 reduction;
texture glaze cone 2 oxidation
Photo by Jack Kraig

*Organic imagery is the primary focus
of my work. This vessel is inspired by
the mysterious forces of our planet.
Abstract, geological processes break
the symmetry at the edge of this
bowl. Perhaps a volcano has erupted
and spewed molten lava from below
the earth's crust?*

Angela Mellor
Glacial Light, 1999

2¾ x 4 in. (7 x 10.2 cm)
Slip-cast bone china; paperclay;
textured; cone 7 oxidation
Photo by Isamu Sawar

*The translucency of bone china and
its potential for the transmission of
light captivates me.* Glacial Light *was
inspired by the stark beauty of
Antarctica: the contrasting textural
forms found in nature emphasized
by dazzling light.*

Sheila M. Lambert
Bonaventure, 2002

4 x 7½ x 7½ in. (10.2 x 19 x 19 cm)
Wheel-thrown stoneware; layered high-fire
glazes; bisque cone 04;
glaze cone 10 gas, reduction
Photo by Steve Mann

Catherine Dotson
Tracy Dotson
Untitled, 2001

5 x 12 in. (12.7 x 30.5 cm)
Wheel-thrown stoneware; layered
glazes; wax resist; cone 10, bent
Photo by Tom Mills

Ginny Conrow

Tall Oval Bowl

9 x 8 x 6½ in. (22.9 x 20.3 x 16.5 cm)
Porcelain; crystalline glaze cone 10
Photo by Roger Schreiber

Bonnie Seeman

Green Bowl, 2001

7 x 6 x 6 in. (17.8 x 15.2 x 15.2 cm)
Wheel-thrown and altered porcelain; hand-built;
bisque cone 06; glaze cone 10 oxidation
Photo by artist

Joe Davis
Slip-Carved Bowl #2, 2001

3½ x 5 x 5 in. (8.9 x 12.7 x 12.7 cm)
Wheel-thrown white stoneware, slip carved; glazed;
salt cone 11 wood

*I strive to make pieces which, when
finished, look as fresh as if they had
just risen from the potter's wheel.
Any piece that succeeds in this will
teach us how it came to life.*

Ryan J. Greenheck
Bowl, 2001

Wheel-thrown porcelain; assembled; bisque cone 06;
soda cone 10

Rae Dunn

Trace, 2002

6 x 10 x 10 in. (15.2 x 25.4 x 25.4 cm)
Coil-built stoneware; etched; oxides; glazed; cone 06

*I don't strive for perfection in line
and form in my work, because the
balance I'm trying to achieve can't
be represented that way.*

Gary Holt
Porcelain Bowl with Drawing, 2001

3½ x 4½ in. (8.9 x 11.4 cm)
Wheel-thrown translucent porcelain; glaze-pencil
drawing; color accents; cone 11 reduction
Photo by Richard Sargent

Louise Rosenfield
Berry Bowl, 2001

3 x 6 in. (7.6 x 15.2 cm)
Wheel-thrown porcelain; carved; pierced; terra sig-
illata; bisque cone 04; glaze cone 10 reduction
Photo by Harrison Evans

Randy Borchers
Pooka Ness

Wave Bowl, 2000

5½ x 6 in. (14 x 15.2 cm)
Wheel-thrown stoneware; carved; glazed; bisque cone
6; glaze cone 9
Photo by Peter Lee

Jenny Mendes
Diamond Head, 2000

15 x 11 x 5½ in. (38 x 28 x 14 cm)
Slab built and slump molded; coiled foot; surface
painted with terra sigilatta; cone 02
Photo by Heather Protz

Susan Kowalczyk
Leaf Bowl, 2000

5½ x 13 x 11½ in. (14 x 33 x 29.2 cm)
Hand-built earthenware; slips; glaze; cone 03
Photo by Andrew Fortune

Shane M. Keena
Untitled

7 x 15 x 15 in. (17.8 x 38.1 x 38.1 cm)
Wheel-thrown porcelain; altered; layered slips; bisque
cone 06; glaze cone 10 reduction
Photo by David Calicchio

Karen A. Case
Orchid Bowl, 2001

5 x 7½ x 6½ in. (12.7 x 19 x 16.5 cm)
Slab built, altered, and drape molded; iron oxide
stain; bisque cone 06; low-fire raku,
newspaper reduction
Photo by Gloria L. Case

Shawn Ireland

Bowl, 2001

12 x 5 in. (30.5 x 12.7 cm)
Slab-built stoneware; raw glazed; rope impressed;
cone 10 wood
Photo by Walker Montgomery

Geoffrey Swindell

Bowl, 2002

3 x 5 in. (7.6 x 12.7 cm)
Wheel-thrown and slip-cast porcelain; incised, gold
leaf interior; cone 7
Photo by Tom Swindell

Traci Beden-Tambussi
Carved Porcelain Bowl, 2000

2¾ x 4½ x 2½ in. (7 x 11.4 x 6.4 cm)
Wheel-thrown porcelain; carved; bisque cone 08;
glaze cone 10 oxidation
Photo by Barbara Hanselman

My first clay teacher taught me to see the beauty in the simple things around us. I believe simplicity is elegance, and I try to show this in my work.

Mary Cay
Pouring Nesters, 2000

Largest: 7½ x 12½ x 12½ in. (19 x 31.8 x 31.8 cm)
Wheel-thrown and altered porcelain; white crackle
glaze; bisque cone 04; glaze cone 10
Photo by Mad Dog Studio

Linda Ganstrom
Prairie Bowl/Dust Bowl, 2002

9 x 22 x 20 in. (22.9 x 55.9 x 50.8 cm)
Double-walled slab-built stoneware; carved; stains;
multi-fired cone 10 wood
Photo by Sheldon Ganstrom

The prairie landscape of Kansas rolls gently, creating soft hills and gentle hollows. The word "prairie" evokes this undulating, sensuous quality, suggestive of fertility and the promise of life and "dust" refers to the more deadly nature of the prairie in drought.

Jerilyn Virden
Untitled (Two-Chambered Bowl), 2002

5½ x 12 x 9 in. (14 x 30.5 x 22.9 cm)
Coil-built stoneware; slab built; hollow form; Barnard-
based glaze; bisque cone 08; glaze cone 10
Photo by Tom Mills

Wolfgang Vegas
In Extinction, 2000

3 x 13¼ x 13¼ in. (7.7
x 33.6 x 33.6 cm)
Slip-cast porcelain in
transform mold; oxides;
underglaze; glaze; glaze
cone 8 electric
Photo by G. Boss

Susan Clusener
Prickly Pair, 1998

Large: 2¾ x 4¾ x 4¾ in. (7 x 12.1 x 12.1 cm);
small: 1¾ x 3 x 3 in. (4.4 x 7.6 x 7.6 cm)
Pinched bowls; pins; oven hardened;
350°F (179°C)
Photo by artist

*Much of my work involves com-
bining various materials with clay.
Currently, I have been integrating
metal, glass, wood, and sand with
clay and glaze, creating different
designs and textures ranging
from inviting to antagonistic.*

Rick Rudd

Bowl, 2001

9¹³⁄₁₆ x 22⁷⁄₁₆ x 15³⁄₈ in. (25 x 57 x 39 cm)
Pinched and coiled terra cotta; scraped; shiny black metallic
glazes; bisque 1742°F (950°C); glaze 2102°F (1150°C)
Photo by Howard Williams

Judith Motzkin
Eggshell Bowl, 1999 *cover*

12 x 11 x 11 in. (30.5 x 27.9 x 27.9 cm)
Wheel-thrown earthenware; terra sigillata; salts;
metals; combustibles; cone 08 gas, saggar-fired
Photo by Dean Powell

Lyn-Rae Ashley
Sun Burst, 2002

Porcelain; burnished; seaweed/sawdust; saggar fired
Photo by David Calicchio

Jeff Kise
Untitled, 2001

7 x 1 ¼ x 11¼ in. (17.8 x 28.5 x 28.5 cm)
Wheel thrown; burnished; low-fire interior; bisque
cone 06; glaze cone 04; saggar fired cone 08
Photo by Tim Barnwell

Una Mjurka
Carrot Bowl #2, 2002

$4\frac{1}{2}$ x 14 x 13 in. (11.4 x 35.6 x 33 cm)
Hand built; layered engobes; oxide; glaze washes;
multi-fired cones 06-04
Photo by artist

Nesrin During *above*

Shell Bowls, 2001

3¾ x 7¾ x 5¾ in. (10 x 18 x 15 cm)
Double-walled, coil-built German Westerwalder clay;
ash glazed; wood/salt 2336–2372°F
(1280–1300°C)
Photo by Stephan During

Gina Freuen *right*

Web-Surfaced Punch Bowl, 2001

13 x 16 x 15 in. (33 x 40.6 x 38.1 cm)
Wheel-thrown porcelainous stoneware; slab built;
textured; stains; clear glaze; bisque cone 04; glaze
cone 6 gas, reduction
Photo by Hamilton Photography

Gay Smith
Jade Bowl, 2001

4 x 8 x 6 in. (10.2 x 20.3 x 15.2 cm)
Wheel-thrown porcelain; altered and faceted on wheel;
trimmed; raw glazed; single-fired soda cone 10

*Although my bowls are more
about an exploration of structure
and surface than about strict
functionality, I trust they will
nourish those who live with them.*

Missy M. McCormick
Small Hollow Walled Service, 2000

3 x 3½ x 3½ in. (7.6 x 8.9 x 8.9 cm)
Wheel-thrown and altered stoneware; double walled;
celedon glaze; bisque cone 06; soda cone 11
cross-draft kiln

Lucy Breslin
Summer Song #12, 2002

11 x 16 x 11 in. (27.9 x 40.6 x 27.9 cm)
Wheel-thrown white earthenware; hand built; layered
glazes; bisque cone 07; glaze cone 04
Photo by Mark Johnson

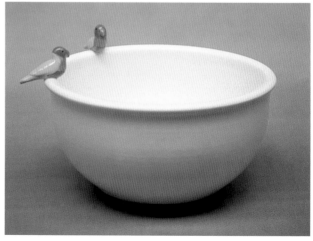

Barbi Lock Lee
Rainbow Lorikeet Bowl, 2001

6 x 9 in. (15.2 x 22.9 cm)
White earthenware
Photo by Ian Hobbs

Geoffrey Wheeler
Oval Bowl, 2000

6 x 18 x 12 in. (15.2 x 45.7 x 30.5 cm)
Wheel-thrown and altered porcelain; slab-built spoons;
glaze cones 6 and 04
Photo by Peter Lee

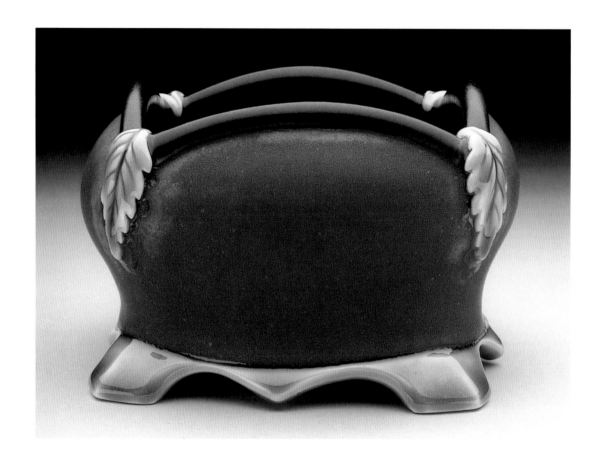

Shannon Nelson
Footed Bowl, 1999

3½ x 5 x 5 in. (8.9 x 12.7 x 12.7 cm)
Slip-cast porcelain; hand built; cone 6 oxidation
Photo by John Knaub

Bryan Hiveley
Ritual Bowl, 2002

Coil built; layered low-fire glazes; cone 04

Rae Dunn

Solace, 2002

6 x 11 x 11 in.
(15.2 x 27.9 x 27.9 cm)
Coil-built stoneware; oxide; glazed; cone 06

Joyce Nagata
Lemons, 1998

14 x 16 x 8 in. (35.6 x 40.6 x 20.3 cm)
Wheel-thrown and altered terra-cotta earthenware;
majolica; bisque cone 04
Photo by John Carlano

Harriet E. Ross
Untitled, 1999

Tallest: 5 x 4 x 3 in. (12.7 x 10.2 x 7.6 cm)
Wheel thrown; cone 10 reduction
Photo by James Dee

Carol Townsend

Patchwork Bowl, 1996

8 x 8 x 9 in. (20.3 x 20.3 x 22.9 cm)
Slab-built stoneware; black and white slip; glazed;
bisque cone 04; glaze cone 6 reduction
Photo by K.C. Kratt

*I am always eager to explore
how the surface pattern
develops a collage-like dia-
logue with the form.*

Juan Granados
Fall Salad Bowl, 2001

4 x 6¾ x 6¾ in. (10.2 x 17.1 x 17.1 cm)
Wheel-thrown and altered porcelain; bisque
cone 08 electric; soda cone 10, reduction
Photo by artist

Ben Carter
Wood-Fired Serving Bowl, 2001

6 x 8 x 6 in. (15.2 x 20.3 x 15.2 cm)
Wheel-thrown stoneware; incised lines on surface;
bisque cone 08; cone 10 wood
Photo by Chris Bledsoe

Jason Bohmert
4 Bowls, 2001

4 x 6 x 6 in. (10.2 x 15.2 x 15.2 cm)
Wheel-thrown and faceted stoneware; slipped;
glazed; cone 11 wood
Photo by artist

*I enjoy making pots that feel
fresh and alive, capturing the
process in the finished piece.
The hand that shaped the pot
should be evident in the pot.*

Jon Arsenault
Shino Tea Bowl, 2000

4½ x 2 x 2 in. (11.4 x 5 x 5 cm)
Wheel-thrown stoneware; shino glaze; cone 10
Photo by Neil Pickett

Marta Matray Gloviczki
Carbon Trap Shino Bowl, 2001

5 x 5 x 5 in. (12.7 x 12.7 x 12.7 cm)
Hand-built porcelain; Davis's Shino glaze;
cone 10 gas
Photo by Peter Lee

Brian Jensen
Untitled, 2002

4 x 4 x 4 in. (10.2 x 10.2 x 10.2 cm)
Stoneware and porcelain; soda
Photo by artist

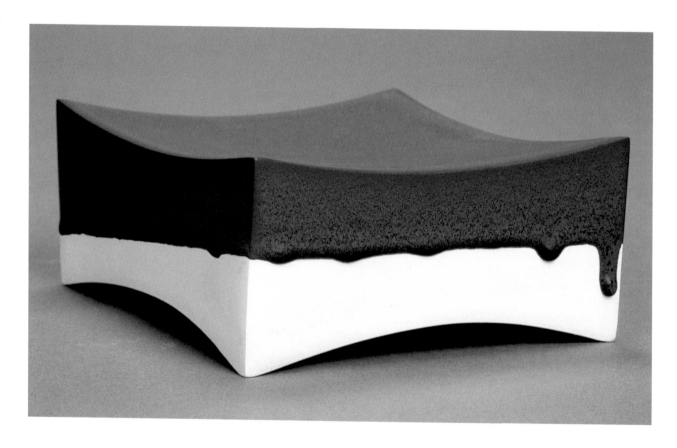

Rachel Leitman
Black and White Bowl, 2001

7 x 7 x 3 in. (17.8 x 17.8 x 7.6 cm)
Slip-cast porcelain; cone 10

Meredith Brickell

Bed, 2001

4 x 16 x 7½ in. (10.2 x 40.6 x 19 cm)
Cast porcelain; unglazed; cone 9 oxidation
Photo by Tom Mills

Callie Morgan *left*
Ram I, 2002

4½ x 5 x 6½ in. (11.4 x 12.7 x 16.5 cm)
Hand-built earthenware; carved; oxides with
Gerstley borate; slips with Mason stains;
bisque cone 04; glaze cone 04
Photo by Mike Noa

Leslie Green below
Fruit Bowl, 2001

3 x 14½ x 2½ in. (7.6 x 36.8 x 6.4 cm)
Slab built; stamped; hump molded; wheel
thrown; cone 6 gas
Photo by Gary G. Gibson

*Clay takes me everywhere.
I'm a happy follower.*

Holly Walker
Untitled, 2000

$3\frac{1}{2}$ x $5\frac{1}{4}$ x $5\frac{1}{4}$ in. (8.9 x 13.3 x 13.3 cm)
Pinched earthenware coils; single fired cone 04
Photo by Tom Mills

Lynn Townson
Bowls with Zigzags and Squares, 2000

3 x 10 in. (7.6 x 25.4 cm)
Wheel-thrown white stoneware; paper resist slip; slip
trailed; bisque cone 06; glaze cone 8 electric

Leslie Thompson
Maori Staircase, 2001

Wheel thrown and carved; black interior glaze;
1800°F (982°C); 2300°F (1260°C)
Photo by Simon Chatwin

Mark Johnson
Bowl with Triangle, 2001

6 x 12 x 12 in. (15.2 x 30.5 x 30.5 cm)
Wheel-thrown white stoneware; wax resist;
multiple glazes; soda cone 10
Photo by artist

*I return to making bowls again and again.
They speak of inherent function and of
the elemental relationship between inside
and outside space.*

Terry Gess
Painted Bowl, 1996

9 x 15 x 15 in. (22.9 x 38.1 x 38.1 cm)
Wheel-thrown white stoneware; multiple slips; salt

Marilyn Dennis Palsha

Spiral Bowl, 2001

3½ x 5 x 5½ in. (8.9 x 12.7 x 14 cm)
Wheel-thrown and altered stoneware;
porcelain slip; oribe; black stain;
bisqued; salt/soda cone 10
Photo by Seth Tice Lewis

Jon Arsenault
Soft Square Bowl, 2001

4 x 4 x 4 in. (10.2 x 10.2 x 10.2 cm)
Wheel-thrown porcelain; altered; sprayed ash glaze;
cone 10
Photo by Tom Mills

D. Hayne Bayless
Bowl with Resist Design, 2001

3½ x 6 x 6 in. (8.9 x 15.2 x 15.2 cm)
Slab-built stoneware; copper glaze; flashing slip;
resist; salt/soda cone 11 wood
Photo by artist

Stephen Mickey
Loaf Bowl, 2002

3 x 4 x 6 in. (7.6 x 10.2 x 15.2 cm)
Wheel-thrown stoneware; altered; shino slip;
anagama fired

Gay Smith
Serving Bowl, 2001

5 x 14 x 9 in. (12.7 x 35.6 x 22.9 cm)
Porcelain; altered and faceted on wheel; added handles;
raw glazed; single fired soda cone 10
Photo by Tom Mills

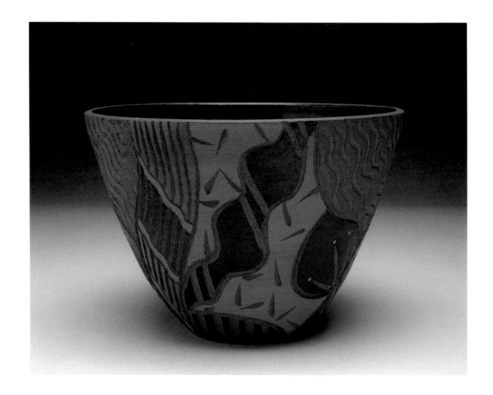

Suzanne Kraman

Bowl, 2000

5 x 5 x 5 in. (12.7 x 12.7 x 12.7 cm)
Wheel thrown; carved; vitreous engobes; bisque cone
06; glaze cone 6 electric, oxidation

*I enjoy working with simple
forms and exploring the division
of surface into a playful array of
color, form, and texture.*

Marysia Gailbraith
Rice Bowl, 2001

3½ x 5 x 5 in. (8.9 x 12.7 x 12.7 cm)
Wheel-thrown red earthenware; incised;
glazed; cone 6 oxidation
Photo by Miyuk Okuyama

Emily Pearlman
Lobed Bowl, 2001

Wheel-thrown stoneware; altered; cut; carved; bisque
cone 06; glaze cone 6 electric
Photo by James Dee

Cathi Jefferson
Rectangle Napper Bowl, 2000

6 x 10 x 12 in. (15.2 x 25.4 x 30.5 cm)
Wheel-thrown and altered porcelainous stoneware;
bottom added; salt/soda cone 10
Photo by John Sinal

Aase Haugaard
Bowls, 1999

12⁹⁄₁₆ x 13¾ in. (32 x 35 cm)
Wheel thrown; slips; salt cone 10

Lis Ehrenreich
Blue Bowl, 2002

5½ x 6¹¹⁄₁₆ in. (14 x 17 cm)
Wheel-thrown red Danish earthenware; stamped;
engobe decorated; bisque 1472°F (800°C);
ash/borax glaze; 2156°F (1180°C) electric, reduction
Photo by Erik Balle Povlsen

Hwang Jeng-Daw
Tea Bowl: Give Me Some Water, 1997

2¾ x 5½ x 4¾ in. (7 x 14 x 12 cm)
Wheel-thrown and altered; black matte and white
shrinkage glazes; cone 8, reduction

Juan Granados
Summer Salad Bowl, 2001

4 x 8 x 8 in. (10.2 x 20.3 x 20.3 cm)
Wheel-thrown and altered porcelain; bisque cone
08; electric cone 10, reduction
Photo by artist

Francois Ruegg

Moon Bowl, 1993

4⅜ x 5⅞ x 5⅞ in. (11 x 15 x 15 cm)
Slip-cast bone china; bisque cones 018 and 08;
black enamel; glaze cone 7
Photo by M. Chollet

Gabriele Hain
Bowl with Three Pierced Rings and
  Four Circles, 1992-1994

2⅛ x 5⅛ x 5⅛ in. (5.5 x 13.1 x 13.1 cm)
Slip-cast Limoges porcelain; pierced and carved;
bisque cone 018, 1436°F (780°C); bisque cone 08;
glaze cone 7, 2246°F (1230°C)
Photo by Franz Linschinger

*Working on the verge of
limits and breakage is
exciting and demanding.*

Lea Zoltowski

Hollow-Rim Bowl, 2001

8¾ x 19¾ in.
(22.2 x 50.2 cm)
Wheel-thrown grolleg porcelain; assembled; zinc silicate crystalline glaze; cone 9 oxidation; controlled cooling
Photo by artist

I draw great inspiration from the patterning and structures seen in nature. I am interested in stretching the material limits of clay and glazes.

Jessica Wilson

Untitled, 2002

6 x 16½ x 16 in.
(15.2 x 41.9 x 40.6 cm)
Wheel-thrown stoneware; assembled; double fired cone 10, reduction

Carol-Ann Michaelson

Untitled, 2001

5 x 14 x 14 in. (12.7 x 35.6 x 35.6 cm)
Wheel-thrown porcelain; spring wire—cut lip; stamp center;
ash glazes; bisque cone 06; glaze cone 08 electric
Photo by Craig Parker

David L. Warren
Blue Bowl #1, 2001

6¾ x 7½ x 7½ in. (17.2 x 19 x 19 cm)
Slab built; hand built; glazed; gold leaf overlay;
cone 04
Photo by Lynn Lockwood

*My work is about the exploration of
form and surface, the ambiguity of
form as object/object as form, and
pushing the boundaries of functionality and art.*

Priscilla Hollingsworth
Licked Leaf Bowl, 2002

6 x 11 x 11 in. (15.2 x 27.9 x 27.9 cm)
Hand-built terra cotta; double walled; applied decora-
tion; underglaze and glaze; cone 04 oxidation
Photo by artist

Jonathan Kaplan
Footed Cone Bowl, 1999

15 x 13 in. (38.1 x 33 cm)
Slip-cast terra cotta; glaze, underglaze;
pigment; cone 4
Photo by David C. Holloway

Marilyn Richeda

Lime Green Bowl, 2001

3 x 6½ x 6½ in. (7.6 x 16.5 x 16.5 cm)
Slab-built red earthenware over bisqued molds;
Mason stains; single-fired cone 04 gas
Photo by Smith-Baer, Ltd.

Patterns, color, and texture are used in my low-fire terra-cotta forms. I really enjoy painting on them. Reaching for the right brush is a mindful moment. I use glazes, slips, and underglazes, and I always brush onto raw clay. I typically fire work two and sometimes three times to achieve the varied layered patterns that seem right to me.

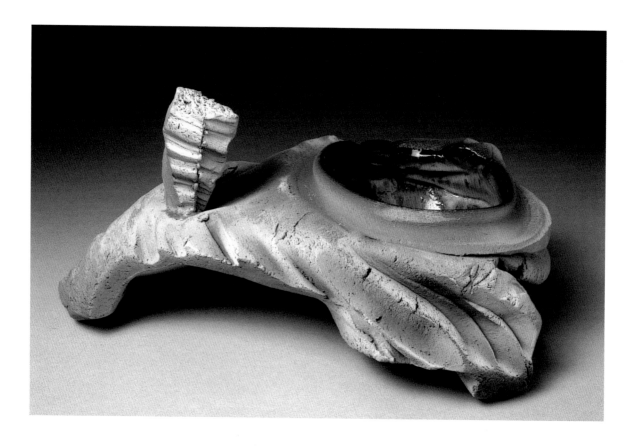

Scott Place
Bowl Form, 2000

5 x 12 x 6 in. (12.7 x 30.5 x 15.2 cm)
Wheel-thrown and altered earthenware; carved; glaze;
underglaze; cone 04 oxidation

Chris Stanley
Party Boy, 1999

6 x 18 x 18 in. (15.2 x 45.7 x 45.7 cm)
Slip-cast porcelain; black, pink engobe; hand
drawings; cut stencils; cone 10
Photo by Eric R. Johnson
Courtesy of John Michael Kohler Art Center

Neville French

Helmet Bowls, 1998

$3\frac{1}{2}$ x $7\frac{7}{8}$ x $6\frac{11}{16}$ in. (9 x 20 x 17 cm)
Wheel-thrown and altered porcelain; layered colored
matte glazes; multi-fired cone 11, 2282°F (1250°C)
Photo by Terence Bogue

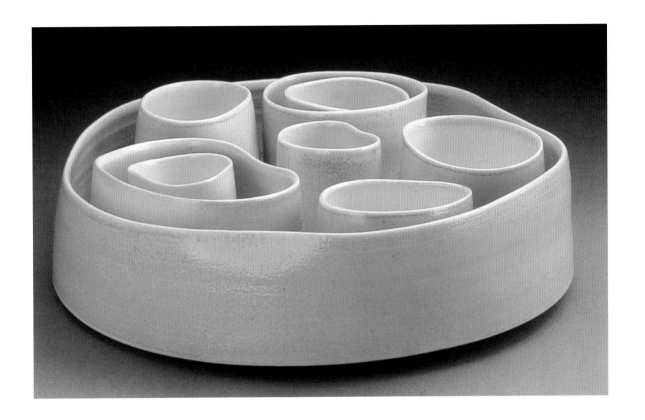

Meredith Brickell

Pools, 2001

Largest: 2½ x 9 x 9 in. (6.4 x 22.9 x 22.9 cm)
Wheel-thrown porcelain; white glaze;
salt cone 10, reduction
Photo by Tom Mills

Jenny Lou Sherburne
Fruit Bowl Set on Stand, 1999

18 x 24 x 14 in. (45.7 x 61 x 35.6 cm)
Wheel-thrown, hand-built, and altered white earthen-
ware; engobes and glaze-carved; cones 04 and 06
Photo by Steve Meltzer

Greg Daly
Tripod Bowl with Enamel & Gold, Silver Leaf, 1999

13⅜ in. (34 cm) diameter
Thrown and cut; oxidation 2372°F (1300°C);
glaze-on-glaze chrome-based enamel and gold and
silver leaf 1364°F (740°C)

Marge Marks

Untitled Bowl, 1999

6½ x 2½ in. (16.5 x 6.4 cm)
Wheel-thrown white stoneware; glaze
inlay; glaze cone 10
Photo by David Calicchio

Sean Miller

Large Bowl, 2001

5⅞ x 11½ x 5⁵⁄₁₆ in. (15 x 29 x 13.5 cm)
Wheel-thrown red clay from Fremington,
Devon, England; slip trailed, poured,
dipped; cone 05
Photo by Stephen Brayne

*These functional ceramics for domestic
use were inspired by traditional European
slipware and folk pottery.*

Matthew A. Yanachuk
Donut Bowl, 2002

5½ x 11 in. (14 x 27.9 cm)
Slip cast; wax-resist

Blaine Avery
Fish Platter–Bowl, 2001

3½ x 18 x 18 in. (8.9 x 45.7 x 45.7 cm)
Shino glaze; slip trailed; cone 10 reduction
Photo by Seth Tice-Lewis

Linda Arbuckle
Square Bowl: Winter, 2001

8½ x 8 in. (21.6 x 20.3 cm)
Wheel-thrown and altered terra cotta;
majolica; cone 03
Photo by Randy Battista/Media Image Photography

McKenzie Smith

Pentagon Bowl, 1999

6 x 6 x 6 in. (15.2 x 15.2 x 15.2 cm)
Stoneware; cone 10 wood
Photo by artist

Steven Roberts
Red Bowl, 2001

3½ x 6 in. (8.9 x 15.2 cm)
Wheel-thrown and altered porcelain; cone 10

Bonnie Seeman Plantation, Florida
Pages 11, 174, 342

Ljubov Seidl Waterfall, New South Wales, Australia
Pages 165, 192

Carol Selfridge Edmonton, Alberta, Canada
Pages 140, 292

Richard Selfridge Edmonton, Alberta, Canada
Pages 140, 292

Stephen Sell Pittsburgh, Pennsylvania
Page 82

Julie Sewell Roswell, Georgia
Page 335

Deborah Shapiro Tigard, Oregon
Pages 77, 299

Lois Sharpe Durham, North Carolina
Page 88

Patricia Shaw Chapel Hill, North Carolina
Page 135

Sharon Shen San Antonio, Texas
Page 295

Jenny Sherburne Lou Gulfport, Florida
Pages 182, 193, 404

Lindy Shuttleworth New York, New York
Page 207

Inguna Skuja Redwood, Oregon
Pages 240, 320

Collette L. Smith Fairfield, Connecticut
Pages 152, 225

Gay Smith Bakersville, North Carolina
Pages 22, 362, 385

Marcia Smith Madison, Wisconsin
Pages 133, 232

McKenzie Smith Dade City, Florida
Pages 278, 410

Wesley L. Smith Lubbock, Tennessee
Page 264

Ian Stainton State College, Pennsylvania
Page 162

Chris Stanley Odessa, Texas
Pages 233, 401

Janice Strawder Philadelphia, Pennsylvania
Page 121

Marvin Sweet Merrimac, Massachusetts
Page 209

Geoffrey Swindell Vale of Glamorgan, United Kingdom
Pages 48, 301, 352

Sarah Tanner Penzance, Cornwall, England
Page 128

Beth J. Tarkington Marietta, Georgia
Page 235

Robin C. Teas Augusta, West Virginia
Page 51

Judy Thompson Kansas City, Missouri
Page 119

Julie Thompson San Diego, California
Pages 148, 240

Leslie Thompson Ojai, California
Pages 76, 308, 381

Cheryl Toth Somersworth, Montana
Page 216

Carol Townsend Snyder, New York
Page 371

Lynn Townson Portland, Oregon
Page 380

Gerbi Tsesarskaia Bay Harbor Island, Florida
Page 288

Joan Ulrich Brooklyn, New York
Page 256

Wolfgang Vegas Yverdon-les-Bains, Switzerland
Pages 215, 356

Marc Verbruggen Antwerp, Belgium
Page 298

Claire Verkoyen Amsterdam, Netherlands
Page 229

Jerilyn Virden Penland, North Carolina
Pages 43, 190, 355

Holly Walker Burnsville, North Carolina
Pages 154, 259, 379

Mark Walnoch Aberdeen, New Jersey
Pages 146, 326

David L. Warren El Prado, New Mexico
Page 396

Cindy Watson Roswell, Florida
Pages 274, 314

Deborah J. Weinstein Loxahatchee, Florida
Page 139

Geoffrey Wheeler Menomonie, Wisconsin
Pages 75, 296, 365

Jake Willson Ojo Sarco, New Mexico
Page 39

Jessica Wilson Aberdeen, New Jersey
Pages 102, 394

Paul Winspear Golden Bay, New Zealand
Page 86

Suzanne Wolfe Honolulu, Hawaii
Page 91

Cheryl Wolff Walnut Creek, California
Page 260

Mandy Wolpert Sydney, New South Wales, Australia
Page 283

Pamela Wood Ridgewood, New Jersey
Page 68

Lyn R. Woods San Antonio, Texas
Page 178

Matthew A. Yanachuk New York, New York
Pages 111, 285, 407

Jennifer Amy Yates Portland, Oregon
Pages 79, 84

Theresa Yondo Novelty, Ohio
Pages 26, 309

Gloria Young Wellington, New Zealand
Pages 110, 325

Maggie Zerafa Sleat, Isle Of Skye, Scotland
Page 117

Lea Zoltowski Newcastle, Maine
Pages 102, 218, 394